Chariot Racing
in the Roman Empire

Chariot Racing in the Roman Empire

FIK MEIJER

TRANSLATED BY LIZ WATERS

The Johns Hopkins University Press

Baltimore

Originally published as *Wagenrennen: Spektakelshows in Rome en Constantinopel*
© 2004 by Fik Meijer, Amsterdam, Athenaeum—Polak & Van Gennep.

Publication has been made possible with financial support from the Dutch
Foundation for Literature.

The Johns Hopkins University Press
2715 North Charles Street
Baltimore, Maryland 21218-4363
www.press.jhu.edu

Library of Congress Cataloging-in-Publication Data

Meijer, Fik.
    Chariot racing in the roman empire / Fik Meijer ; translated by Liz Waters.
        p.   cm.
    Includes bibliographical references and index.
    ISBN-13: 978-0-8018-9697-2 (hardcover : alk. paper)
    ISBN-10: 0-8018-9697-5 (hardcover : alk. paper)
    1. Horse racing—History. 2. Rome—Civilization. I. Waters, Liz. II. Title.
    GV33.M45 2010
    798.400937—dc22   2009052698

A catalog record for this book is available from the British Library.

*Special discounts are available for bulk purchases of this book. For more information,
please contact Special Sales at 410-516-6936 or specialsales@press.jhu.edu.*

The Johns Hopkins University Press uses environmentally friendly book materials,
including recycled text paper that is composed of at least 30 percent post-consumer waste,
whenever possible. All of our book papers are acid-free, and our jackets and covers are
printed on paper with recycled content.

For my five little hobbyhorse drivers

Bram, Pim, and Teun (b. 12 August 2001)
Pelle (b. 29 August 2002)
Loet (b. 19 September 2004)

CONTENTS

Acknowledgments   ix
Chronology   xi

Introduction   1

1 The Nika Riot: Thirty Thousand Dead in
the Hippodrome   5

2 Chariot Races of the First Century BC and Earlier   14

3 The Circus Maximus   32

4 Preparation and Organization   52

5 A Day at the Circus Maximus   65

6 The Heroes of the Arena   82

7 The Spectators   96

8 Changes around the Racetrack   128

9 The Heroes of the Hippodrome   141

10 The Disappearance of Chariot Racing   150

11 *Ben-Hur:* Chariot Racing in the Movies   154

List of Racetracks   161
Notes   163
Glossary   171
Selected Bibliography   173
Index   177

ACKNOWLEDGMENTS

I would like to thank Mark Pieters and Susan Breeuwsma of Athenaeum—Polak & Van Gennep publishers for the inspiring and warmhearted way in which they saw the Dutch edition of this book through to publication. I found their critical approach extremely stimulating. My thanks also to Vincent Hunink for his valuable support. Eric Moormann, with his extensive knowledge of iconography, helped me greatly in choosing appropriate illustrations.

Second millennium BC	Battle chariots in use in Greece and the Near East
Eighth century BC	Homer describes chariot racing
776 BC	First Olympic Games
753 BC	Founding of Rome; beginning of the time of the kings
After 753 BC	Rape of the Sabines in the valley between the Aventine and Palatine hills
680 BC	Chariot racing on the Olympic program
c. 600 BC	Tarquinius Priscus starts building the Circus Maximus
530–520 BC	First depictions of teams of horses in the Italian peninsula
509 BC	Beginning of the Republic
366 BC	First officially recorded *ludi*
328 BC	Starting gates built at the Circus Maximus
264–241 BC	First Punic War
218–201 BC	Second Punic War
196 BC	Embellishment of the Circus Maximus
186 BC	Fulvius Nobilior organizes the first wild beast hunt in the Circus Maximus

149–146 BC	Third Punic War
45 BC	Julius Caesar expands the Circus Maximus to seat 150,000
31 BC	Fire at the Circus Maximus
27 BC–14 AD	Augustus, the first emperor
14–37 AD	Tiberius
37–41	Caligula
41–54	Claudius
46	Number of races per day fixed at twenty-four
54–68	Nero
69	Galba, Otho, and Vitellius
69–79	Vespasian
79–81	Titus
79	Eruption of Vesuvius
81–96	Domitian
98–117	Trajan
c. 100	The Circus Maximus reaches its maximum size
117–38	Hadrian
122–146	Diocles triumphs in the Circus Maximus
136–61	Antoninus Pius
161–80	Marcus Aurelius
180–92	Commodus
193–211	Septimius Severus
204	Major "centenary festival," or *ludi saeculares*
211–17	Caracalla
235–38	Maximinus the Thracian

244–49	Philippus the Arab
276–82	Probus
284–305	Diocletian
306–12	Maxentius
306–37	Constantine
354	Calendar of Philocalus, showing holidays for theatrical performances, chariot races, and gladiator shows
379–95	Theodosius I
395–408	Arcadius
408–50	Theodosius II
450–57	Marcian
457–74	Leo I
474	Leo II
474–91	Zeno
491–518	Anastasius
500–540	Porphyrius, Constantinus, Julianus, Faustinus, and Uranius triumph at the Hippodrome in Constantinople
518–27	Justin I
527–65	Justinian
532	Nika riot
549	Last chariot races in Rome
565–78	Justin II
578–83	Tiberius II Constantine
Seventh century onward	Decline in the popularity of chariot races

1204   Constantinople conquered by the Venetians

1453   Constantinople conquered by the Turks; end of
the Byzantine Empire

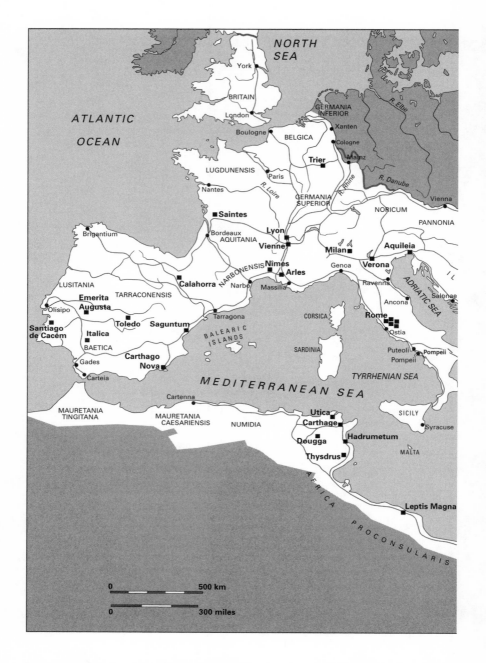

Most important circuses of the Roman Empire in the imperial era. (J. ter Haar)

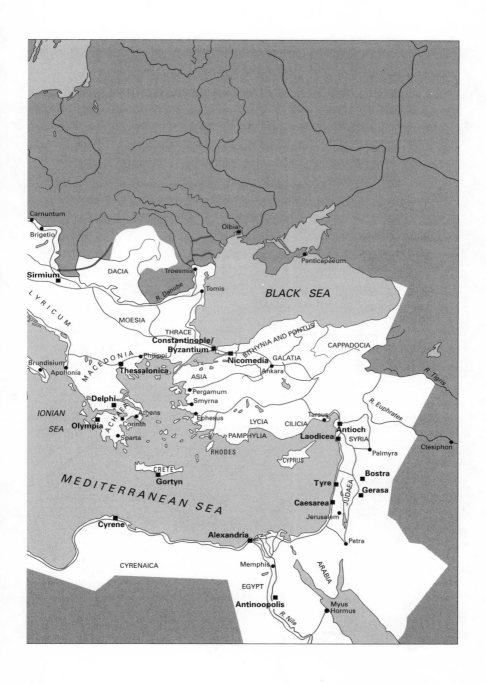

Carnuntum
Brigetio
Sirmium
LYRICUM
DACIA
Troesmis
R. Danube
Tornis
BLACK SEA
Olbia
Panticapaeum
MOESIA
THRACE
Constantinople/
Byzantium
BITHYNIA AND PONTUS
CAPPADOCIA
MACEDONIA
Philippi
Nicomedia
GALATIA
Brundisium
Apollonia
Thessalonica
ASIA
Ankara
R. Tigris
Delphi
Pergamum
Smyrna
R. Euphrates
IONIAN
SEA
Olympia
ACHAEA
Athens
Corinth
Sparta
Ephesus
LYCIA
CILICIA
Tarsus
PAMPHYLIA
Antioch
Laodicea
SYRIA
Palmyra
Ctesiphon
RHODES
CYPRUS
CRETE
Gortyn
Bostra
MEDITERRANEAN SEA
Tyre
Gerasa
Caesarea
JUDAEA
Jerusalem
Cyrene
Alexandria
Petra
CYRENAICA
Memphis
ARABIA
EGYPT
Antinoopolis
Myus
Hormus
R. Nile

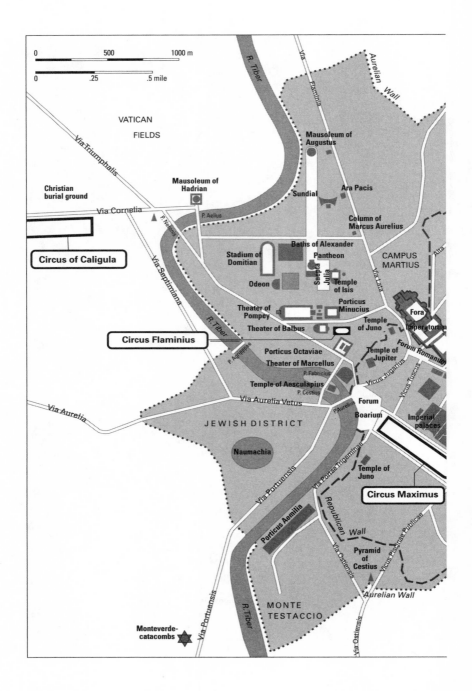

Ancient Rome

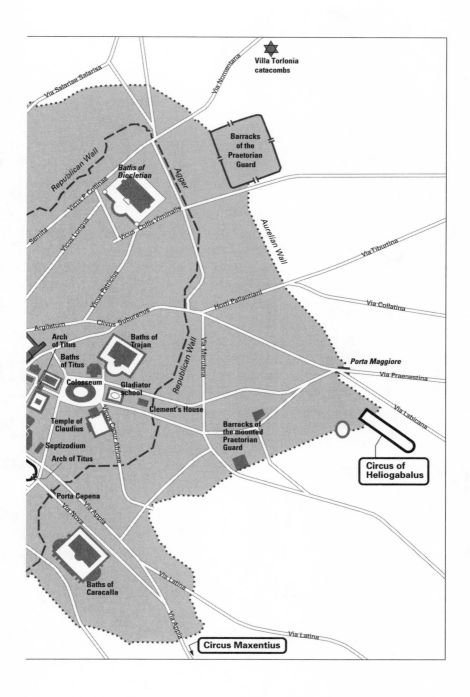

Chariot Racing
in the Roman Empire

Introduction

Panem et circenses (bread and circuses). It was the poet Juvenal who gave us that famous, often quoted phrase. In his opinion a great many people in Rome were interested in only two things: free handouts of bread, and chariot races in the Circus Maximus.[1] The provision of grain has been described and analyzed at length in contemporary studies, whereas chariot races have received less than their fair share of attention. The number of monographs on the subject is limited,[2] and the races occupy no more than a few paragraphs in handbooks on ancient history, slotted in next to that other form of entertainment, the gladiator shows.

This scant degree of interest is remarkable because the chariot races in the Circus Maximus captivated just about the entire population. On festival days some 150,000 fans from every social stratum passed through the gates. Emperors, senators, knights, and governors of provincial cities spent the whole day in the company of ordinary citizens, freedmen, and slaves, enthusiastically watching a sport that could undoubtedly be called the greatest of Roman passions.

For ordinary people the Circus Maximus was a place where they put their daily concerns out of their mind and briefly forgot how insignificant they were in the Roman social hierarchy. For the emperor the Circus Maximus had a special significance. Here he stood eye to eye with his people. As soon as he entered, he could gauge his popularity from the noise up in the stands. Cheers and jeers were the crowd's way of letting him know what they thought of him, and in that sense the Circus Maximus functioned as a political barometer. After the official people's assemblies were stripped of their powers at the beginning of the imperial era, it became the only place where ordinary folk could make their voices heard.

The fact that the elite and the common people of Rome came to watch chariot races together in the Circus Maximus is really rather extraordinary, since in normal life a huge gulf separated them. Outside the stadium, aristocrats displayed nothing but contempt for ordinary people and had nothing good to say about their occupations and pastimes. They made clear to the populace on an almost daily basis that they themselves led very different lives, making far better use of their time in ways that befitted their status. They were proud to have succeeded in striking a proper balance between public life and private pursuits. They could satisfy their political aspirations in the Senate, but since being a senator was not a full-time job, they had plenty of hours to spend on other activities, whether sporting or intellectual. Leading figures who violated the prevailing norms and indulged in excessive greed, indolence, and idleness were reprimanded, since a life that did not match the criteria the elite had formulated for itself was a life not worth living. Intellectuals were especially trenchant in their criticism of useless pastimes, dismissing them as unbecoming to the status of a truly free man. They extolled the virtues of a markedly different existence, one with a central place reserved for science, literature, and the fine arts.

Intellectuals could muster neither sympathy nor understanding for the lower orders and made no imaginative effort to put themselves in their place, simply seeing the plebeians as inferior, incapable of making any real contribution to the state, as people who could not even pay their way but relied for their daily sustenance on the distribution of free grain or on subsidies from the emperor. To cap it all, the townsfolk took pleasure in ephemeral amusements. Some among the intellectual elite even advocated minimizing contact with the masses to avoid being diverted from their own moral standards. They drew a dividing line to separate themselves, with their high status, from the lowly, contemptible people who lived in poverty and could think of nothing better to do than loiter in bars and hang about inside or outside the Circus Maximus and the Colosseum.

Given that this way of thinking was prevalent among the upper echelons of Roman society, it is difficult initially to comprehend why so many of their number abandoned themselves to this particular form of mass entertainment. Looked at realistically, their doing so is not surprising at all. Chariot races were an astonishing phenomenon. They stirred excitement and triggered emotions that few could suppress. The elite succumbed to the atmosphere like everyone else, to the thrills and competitiveness between the walls of the Circus Maximus. Condescending comments from a few opponents of chariot racing stand in sharp contrast to the fervor of the majority. No matter how often Seneca, Pliny the Younger, and Tacitus wrote that chariot races aroused only the most primitive feelings in people, they were ignored. Many Roman aristocrats went along to the Circus Maximus and shouted for their favorite charioteers just as fanatically as the common people did.

What they rarely did, if at all, was write about chariot racing. As authors they cultivated the impression that they appreciated only spiritually uplifting amusements and disapproved of all the diversions enjoyed by ordinary people. This ambivalence, this grappling by the elite with a form of popular entertainment that on ideological grounds they could only look down on yet which gave many of them enormous pleasure, makes chariot racing a particularly fascinating subject today. It becomes even more intriguing when we realize that the vast majority of the charioteers who fired the enthusiasm of spectators were slaves or freedmen, with an even lower status than ordinary folk. Charioteers must have produced some truly extraordinary performances to transform themselves into popular heroes despite this status handicap. Even people who had no interest in chariot racing would have been forced to admit that the utmost skill, dexterity, coolness, patience, and concentration were demanded of the drivers of four-horse teams and that these men were putting into practice the old Roman virtues of dauntlessness, tenacity, and courage. True, a tiny minority, a conservative, purely intellectually inclined segment of the elite, did not regard even all these qualities combined as reason enough to say anything positive about chariot racing. The majority ignored their disapproval, however, throwing themselves into the pandemonium of the Circus Maximus with utter abandon, cheering on their favorites side by side with the common folk and the emperor. Rome was briefly united; all its class differences briefly fell away. But when evening came and the show was over, the old dividing lines were drawn again, and traditional relationships were restored.

Chariot races, both the sport and its social and political background, are the subject of this book. My story is dominated by Rome, but Constantinople is very much part of the picture. In the fourth century it became the new Rome, taking over not just the political power of the old capital but the great popular entertainment of charioteering.

CHAPTER 1

The Nika Riot

Thirty Thousand Dead
in the Hippodrome

Constantinople, early January AD 532. In the "New Rome," founded by Emperor Constantine in 330, there was a palpable sense of unrest. Justinian, who had now ruled the Byzantine Empire for nearly five years, had failed to convince the residents of the city their interests were in good hands. He had completely destroyed his relationship with the members of the old aristocracy, who believed Justinian had gone too far in curtailing their powers. They were joined in their criticism by townsfolk and farmers who were angry at the emperor for raising taxes drastically and who expressed their rage in mass disturbances of the peace. Gangs rampaged through the city, looting and vandalizing. Justinian was unable to stem the violence. The tension reached fever pitch, brawls and arson became the order of the day, and entire districts of the city were reduced to rubble. The response from the emperor was a long time in coming, but when it finally came, it was devastating: on Monday, 19 January 532, more than thirty thousand people were killed in the Hippodrome.

It was far from incidental that the bloodbath took place in the Hippodrome. The people of Constantinople were treated to thrilling chariot races there on seventy days a year. The audience watched breathlessly as four-horse chariots tore around a track more than five hundred meters long and a hundred meters wide. The Hippodrome had been built by Emperor Septimius Severus in the early third century, when the city was still called Byzantium, and Emperor Constantine had expanded and embellished it when he founded his new city. It was more than simply an arena where people gathered to watch chariot racing. Like the Circus Maximus in Rome, the Hippodrome was a place where all segments of the population made their grievances known to the emperor and showed him the extent of his popularity. With its tiers of seating for up to eighty thousand spectators, it was an impressive structure, built high on a hill right in the center of the city, close to the royal palace. The emperor sat near the middle, in his emperor's loge (*kathisma*), a kind of balcony that he could reach directly by a flight of steps from his imperial palace. Around him sat the senators on marble seats, and higher up were the rest of the crowd on tiers of simpler seating.

The massacre in the Hippodrome was the disastrous closing chapter to a week of unprecedented chaos and conflict in the city center. On Tuesday, 13 January, six days before the carnage, the Hippodrome was the scene of serious disturbances. The spectators let fly at each other in the stands, and Justinian was unable to find an approach that would calm them down. Fighting and disorder were not uncommon in the Hippodrome. In the two centuries since the founding of Constantinople, there had been several occasions when riots broke out in and around the racetrack, but they had usually been put down fairly promptly, sometimes without bloodshed, sometimes with multiple fatalities. This time the violence seemed impossible to curtail, even though the causes were no different in essence than they were on previous occasions. As was almost always the case, the trouble stemmed from the great rivalry between groups of supporters of the two main stables, the Greens and the Blues, who, dressed in their club colors, were in the habit of hurling the most frightful abuse at each other.

The riots of 13 January were a discharge of tensions between Greens and Blues that had been building to a climax over several weeks. Vendettas were played out everywhere, both in the Hippodrome and in the densely populated urban districts outside. The city militia mobilized repeatedly to restore order, but to no avail. Emperor Justinian was powerless to act, partly because of his innate hesitancy but, more important, because he had openly sided with the Blues. Every time he made a move against the Greens, they interpreted it as favoritism toward their opponents.

A few days before the eruption of violence, the Greens indulged in an outburst of emotion during the chariot races. In their anger and frustration they yelled that the Blues were being shown preferential treatment to a scandalous extent. The emperor did not deign to re-

Emperor Justinian in a mosaic in the San Vitale in Ravenna. (The Yorck Project)

spond to their reproaches personally but left the job to an envoy, whose attempts to deflect criticism with counteraccusations only enflamed the Greens' rage even further. The tension was wound up tighter still when the spokesman for the Greens made it known that yet another of their number had been murdered, the twenty-sixth in a mere few months. When he laid the blame for the killing on Justinian, the Blues, up in arms, shouted that the only murderers in the Hippodrome were to be found among the Greens. The emperor's herald then added fuel to the fire by accusing the Greens of blasphemy. He called them Jews, Samaritans, and Manichaeans,[1] even asking himself aloud whether they had been baptized. The Greens, insulted, walked out of the stands hurling abuse at the emperor and the Blues.

In the days that followed there was street fighting between Greens and Blues all over the city. The imperial troops put a stop to the trouble, but according to the Greens they exceeded their authority in doing so and proved they were prejudiced by going after them alone and sparing the Blues. The Greens were increasingly intractable, and large numbers turned violent, both in the streets and in the Hippodrome during the races. When the Blues responded to provocation, the emperor had no choice but to intervene with force against his own side. He sent police to deal with the rioters. An unknown number of people, both Greens and Blues, were arrested and imprisoned. Seven were accused of murder and condemned to death. Four were beheaded immediately while the other three were sentenced to be hanged, but two, a Green and a Blue, escaped the death penalty when the nooses did not work properly and they fell down onto the scaffold. They were taken away by monks from a nearby monastery and given asylum in the Church of St. Lawrence, but the city prefect refused to resign himself to this outcome and cordoned off the church. Then something happened that has a way of happening in our own time: the ringleaders of the Greens and the Blues called off their battle, and together they turned on the police, although they did not succeed in rescuing their fellow supporters.

On Tuesday, 13 January, Emperor Justinian acted as if nothing had happened. He simply went ahead and held chariot races. Perhaps he felt the situation was not particularly explosive, but it is equally likely that he considered it important not to give the troublemakers the idea they could throw everything into disorder. After a fractious day in the Hippodrome, during the twenty-second of the twenty-four races, all the supporters' frustrations surfaced. Both Greens and Blues began asking the emperor to grant clemency to the two supporters who had found refuge in St. Lawrence's Church, but Justinian ignored them and simply refused to respond to their entreaties. To a man the spectators chanted "*nika, nika*" ("conquer, conquer," the cry that usually went up as the crowd cheered on the drivers during the races), and "long live the Blues and the Greens!" The emperor must have felt extremely uncomfortable. He was at a loss as to how to deal with the situation, and he fled through the special lockable passageway from his loge into the palace.

That evening Greens and Blues marched en masse to the palace of the city prefect and demanded the release of the prisoners. Receiving no answer, they moved on to the prison, forced their way in, and freed all the offenders held there. In an invincible rage they proceeded to the imperial palace and set fire to it. Not even the Hagia Sophia (Church of St. Sophia), built there by Emperor Constantine, was spared. It was lost to the flames.

Justinian continued to underestimate the seriousness of the situation. The following morning he allowed the chariot races planned for that day to go ahead. Perhaps he was hoping that the love of the Greens and Blues for the races would outweigh their rage, but he was wrong. When the racing began, there was no holding the spectators, who set light to the stands. The fire spread to the public Baths of Zeuxippus next door, reducing them to charred ruins.

The rioters quickly gained in self-confidence, especially when they began receiving mass support from dissatisfied farmers in the surrounding countryside. The freeing of the prisoners had become a side issue to the enraged supporters; they were now demanding the resignation of the magistrates, whom they held responsible for the disarray. Justinian, at his wits' end, complied with their request, but despite this concession he was unable to restore law and order. The riots became even more aggressive and violent, the emperor even more indecisive.

The infuriated supporters could tell he was no longer in command of the situation and might bow to pressure at any moment. On Thursday, 15 January, shouting slogans such as "We want a different emperor for the city," they set off for the palace of Probus, a nephew of the previous emperor, Anastasius, intending to proclaim him emperor. Fearing the rage of the populace, however, Probus had already left his house and gone into hiding. So the mob turned its fury on him, too, and set his palace alight before spreading out across the city, looting and burning as it went.

On Friday, 16 January, the chaos reached a new climax. The entire area around the Hagia Sophia was burned to the ground by rioters. The city's police headquarters was among the buildings that fell to the frenzy of the insurrectionists. And still no answer came from the emperor. Justinian finally responded on Saturday, 17 January. Loyal Thra-

Empress Theodora in a mosaic in the San Vitale in Ravenna. (The Yorck Project)

cian troops entered the city and engaged the Blues and Greens in battle, but in the narrow streets and alleyways of Constantinople there was little they could do to defeat the rioters. They were forced to withdraw to barracks adjacent to the imperial palace.

Crisis talks in the palace followed. Justinian now realized that if he could not put an end to the riots his fate was sealed. The following day, Sunday, 18 January, more chariot races were due to take place in the Hippodrome. Justinian took his seat in the emperor's loge with the Gospels under his arm, presumably to give the supporters tangible evidence that he was feeling merciful and that he regretted some of his decisions of the past few days. Nevertheless, only a tiny minority of the supporters cheered their emperor, shouting slogans like "Justinian, may you triumph." Everyone else greeted him with cries of "You're breaking your oaths of allegiance, scoundrel." Justinian was distraught. He rushed out of the Hippodrome in a panic.

Powerless and desperate, Justinian sent home everyone he did not completely trust, including Hypatius and Pompeius, nephews of his predecessor Anastasius. The historian Procopius, who reports these events, does not tell us whether the emperor removed them because he was afraid they were up to something and suspected the rebels wanted one or another of them on the throne or whether it was pure chance, given that they were dismissed along with a large number of senators. The plan probably originated with Justinian's wife, Theodora, who was the daughter of a bear tamer and a circus acrobat and until her marriage a successful variety artist. She had a reputation as a resolute, tough, and at the same time intelligent woman who was far from easily flustered.

When on the early morning of Monday, 19 January, the people found out that Hypatius and Pompeius had been dismissed by Justinian, they went looking for Hypatius to proclaim him emperor. He showed no great enthusiasm. His wife rejected the plan outright, and when the rebels came to fetch Hypatius, she tried to stop him from leaving, bursting into tears and saying he was going to his doom. Nothing she said did any good. The crowd took her husband away and proclaimed him their emperor in the Forum of Constantine.

Meanwhile, talks in the palace continued. Some people, including Emperor Justinian, wanted to flee to the harbor and seek safety elsewhere, taking bags full of money with them, but Empress Theodora refused to yield. In a fiery speech she argued that it was simply not fitting for an empress, once she had been invested and had worn the purple, to run away. She made it very clear to the emperor that if he wanted to flee he would have to go alone. He had plenty of money, the sea was open, and ships lay ready in the harbor. She would not accompany him on his humiliating retreat. For her there was only one path to take, that of confrontation, even if it led to her downfall. She managed to convince the emperor. At last he decided to mount an attack on the rebels. His trusted generals Belisarius and Mundus were ordered to send troops to eliminate the ringleaders.

Meanwhile the insurrectionists had gathered in the Hippodrome, where they intended to ratify Hypatius's appointment formally. The stadium was full, almost to capacity. The atmosphere was nervous, the tension palpable. Did those present know they had gone too far and that a response from the emperor was inevitable? The Blues began to regret the fact that they were joining forces with their archenemies the Greens to appoint a new emperor even though they had always enjoyed Justinian's support. Some simply felt it was wrong; others changed their mind after Narses, a sly eunuch and a confidant of Justinian's, started buying them off. The supporters in the Hippodrome resumed their earlier battle.

Hypatius felt extremely uncomfortable amid supporters' groups that no longer knew what they were doing. His position became untenable when troops suddenly stormed in from two sides. First Belisarius cleared a path through the debris from the western side of the Hippodrome and positioned his men to the right of the emperor's loge, the area occupied by the Blues. He considered taking the *kathisma* immediately and dragging Hypatius out but dismissed that idea and decided to deal with the spectators first. Narses must have done a good job of bribing the Blues, since there was no organized resistance from them at all. At that point Mundus's troops appeared from the other side. The supporters were trapped.

The slaughter that followed, carried out by Justinian's troops, defies description. The few words that Procopius and other writers devote to the bloodbath leave no room for doubt that this was a disaster of unprecedented magnitude. The panic in the Hippodrome was immense; as spectators fled in terror, many fell and were trampled underfoot. Those who managed to get out of the way found the exits blocked. They ran around the arena like hunted animals while the soldiers carried on their lethal work. Anyone who came within range of the soldiers' swords, Green or Blue, was mercilessly hacked down. More than thirty thousand people were killed.[2] It was the biggest supporter bloodbath in history.

The next day Hypatius was executed on Justinian's orders. His defense, that he had wanted none of this, was noted for the record. It was a long time before lasting peace was restored in the city. The Hippodrome remained closed until, after several years had passed, Justinian calculated that he had built up enough credit once again to organize chariot races without the risk of major riots. A few months later he ordered a start to be made on the reconstruction of the ruined city. For Justinian the quashing of the Nika riot was ultimately the start of a period of unbridled construction, with the new Hagia Sophia as the most tangible symbol of the new spirit of the age. The thirty thousand or more fans who had died became a mere footnote in history.

CHAPTER 2

Chariot Races
of the First Century BC
and Earlier

The Prelude

The Nika riot took place at a time when chariot racing had developed into an unparalleled mass spectacle with a rich tradition behind it. At the start it was very different. Chariot races began so modestly that we cannot say with any certainty where and when they were first held. All we can be sure of is that the sport of charioteering was introduced rather sooner in some regions than others, depending on the availability of sufficient horses and large empty fields. In the Middle East, with plenty of wide open spaces, chariot races were no doubt held earlier than in mountainous Greece, but wherever they came about, it was only after people had been using wagons and carts for many years for more practical purposes: moving agricultural produce from their farmland to villages and towns and transporting people and goods over longer distances.

Contrary to what we might perhaps expect, the first vehicles were not pulled by domesticated horses but by pack animals, mainly donkeys and mules. As farms became larger and demand in the cities for their produce increased, carts became more diverse, and oxen were hitched to them as well. Although all these animals were slower than horses, they were preferred for their weight, their stamina, and their steady pace, certainly on the steep and heavily broken ground of Greece, where speed was of secondary importance and there was therefore little to be gained by using horses. A horse was a status symbol, a way for its owner to display his wealth. The mere fact that he owned animals he did not need for economic activity won him respect. Horses were hitched to wagons for other reasons, too, for higher purposes in their

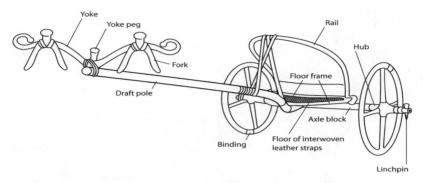

Egyptian war chariot from Thebes of c. 1400 BC, with the most important components marked.

owners' eyes: for wars and for contests between the rich in the form of chariot races.

War chariots were a familiar sight in the Near East in the second millennium BC. The Egyptians, who had probably adopted the concept of the war chariot from the Canaanites, tailored their military tactics to the speed and effectiveness of their vehicles. Under King Thutmose III (1479–1425 BC) the army was made up of infantry units supported on their flanks by war chariots deployed in squadrons of twenty-five. These were lightweight structures on two wheels with four, later sometimes six, spokes.

To the Hittites, whose heartland was in the highlands of Anatolia, war chariots were even more important. Their armies were divided into battalions centered on a large number of chariots, each with a crew of two or three: the driver plus one or two soldiers armed with spears, lances, or javelins. A tough training program was used to select these highly respected elite warriors, and specially bred horses made the chariot into a weapon of war that presented an enormous challenge to an enemy lacking chariots of his own.

Kings in the Middle East flaunted their ownership of huge numbers of war chariots, which they saw as proof of their power, and the Mycenaean kings of Greece in the second millennium were equally proud of their vehicles. Inscriptions on clay tablets tell of a king in Knossos on Crete who had more than four hundred war chariots, and of one ruler of Pylos on the west coast of the Peloponnesos peninsula who

Reconstruction of a Mycenaean battle chariot of c. 1450–200 BC, designed to be drawn by two horses. The second horse is not shown, allowing details of the draft mechanism to be seen.

commanded more than a hundred. Pictures in Mycenaean palaces show fast, slender vehicles, very much like the war chariots of ancient Egypt. It is impossible to know whether they were ever deployed in organized chariot races.

Around 1100 BC a wind of change swept through the Mediterranean world. Invasions by tribes from the north put an end to the dominance of the charioteer peoples. In Asia Minor the Hittite Empire collapsed, and in Greece the Mycenaean civilization vanished. The war chariot lost its military significance and gradually became an exclusive means of rapid transport as members of the elite were driven to the battlefield by charioteers. While their drivers waited in the chariots, aristocratic warriors engaged the enemy in hand-to-hand combat with spears and swords. When the battle was over, they were driven back to their camps. Greek aristocrats became increasingly intrigued by the speed of their war chariots. It dawned on them that chariot races, in which they could compete against each other in light, sleek, two-wheel vehicles, each drawn by a pair of specially bred horses, offered novel possibilities. The extent to which such races grabbed the imagination is clear from the large number of racing chariots depicted in vase paintings of the eighth century BC.

The chariot race described by Homer, as illustrated on the François vase of c. 575 BC. The painter clearly knew the story but not the details, since apart from Diomedes the names on the vase are not those of the competitors in Homer's account. (Photograph by Sailko)

Also dating from this period is the first ever written account of a chariot race, in the twenty-third book of the *Iliad* by Homer.[1] Patroclus, a close friend of Achilles', has been killed by Hector the Trojan, and funeral games are to be held in his honor. The program will include a chariot race between vehicles drawn by pairs of horses. On a field near the coast at Troy, just outside the camp of the assembled Greeks, a course is laid out. A starting line is marked, and after drawing lots, the competitors take up their positions. At the far end of the track a six-foot weather-beaten tree trunk has been set into the ground, and the drivers have to pass around it counterclockwise. White stones flanking the post prevent wheels from being smashed against it in the crush. The great difference between these and later chariot races is that the contestants drive only once around the track. Homer does not tell us the distance. Spectators are barely considered at all; the common people, who have walked to Troy to cheer on their Homeric heroes, sit on a hill behind the starting line. From there they have a good view of the start and the finish, but most of the race takes place a long way off.

Homer's report is not an eyewitness account but a beautifully composed, evocative story. The poet begins by enumerating the prizes to be won: kettles, tripods, horses, cows, mules, slave girls, and valuable iron. He then describes, at some length, the process of drawing lots for the starting order and writes that the name of Antilochus is the first to be pulled out of the helmet, followed by those of Eumelus, Menelaus, Meriones, and, last, Diomedes. Homer has little to say about the start and the first half of the race; all his attention is focused on the denouement in the final few meters.

The way the race is decided in the end may seem strange to us, but Homer's readers were accustomed to the idea that not the participants but the gods would make the decisive moves. They take part in person. When Diomedes' whip is knocked out of his hand by Phoebus Apollo, the goddess Athena intervenes to make sure he gets it back. This is not the end of her involvement. She causes Eumelus's chariot, which is out in front, to crash, so that Diomedes can take the lead. Without any further difficulty, Diomedes races on to victory. A fierce battle for second place develops between Menelaus and Antilochus. The latter takes every conceivable risk, steers his horses dangerously close to the water-filled ditches in the center of the track, and finishes second to Diomedes, whose lead is impossible to make up. Menelaus, cursing and swearing at Antilochus's reckless behavior, comes in third, well ahead of Meriones in fourth place.

Homer's lengthy account indicates that in his time chariot races, far from being unusual, were organized quite regularly and spontaneously, whether on special occasions or as part of ceremonial rites.

Olympic Games

At the time that Homer was writing his epic poems, the Greeks in their independent city-states were beginning to reflect on their shared roots and to organize major festivals. The events in which they expressed their sense of identity most strongly were the great stephanitic games at Olympia, Delphi, Corinth, and Nemea. These were Panhellenic festivals, where Greeks from all points of the compass came together to match themselves against one another at wrestling, boxing, athletics, and chariot racing and later in the skills of rhetoric and musical performance as well. They received only a garland (*stephanos*) for victory; the stephanitic games are therefore sometimes referred to as the "wreath games." The Olympic Games were the most prestigious of the four, and tradition has it that they were first organized in 776 BC in a district called Elis on the Peloponnesos peninsula, at Olympia, which lies at the confluence of the rivers Cladeus and Alpheus. But stories about their beginnings go back much further than that, into the era of myth.

Among the Greeks, various stories circulated about the origin of the games. According to the most ancient myth, they had first been held in the far distant past to commemorate Zeus's overthrow in battle of his father, Cronus. Another version makes a connection between the games and the demigod Herakles, son of Zeus and Alcmene. On the way home after one of his many heroic deeds, Herakles is said to have passed the grave of the hero Pelops and organized games for him there. Pelops himself is the figure most often credited, along with King Oenomaus of Pisa (close to Olympia). This version is supported by a chariot-racing story. Oenomaus had a pretty daughter called Hippodamia ("the horse tamer"). It had once been foretold that Oenomaus's daughter's husband would be responsible for his death, and so to prevent his daughter from marrying, Oenomaus demanded of every prospective bridegroom that he first compete against him in the arena, in a four-horse chariot, or *quadriga*. Thirteen candidates had paid with their lives for attempts to win Hippodameia's hand, but Pelops was undeterred, even though he knew that Oenomaus's horses, given to him by Ares, the god of war, were unbeatable. They could run faster than the north wind. Oenomaus always gave his opponents a good head start, then caught up and speared them to death.

This race turned out differently. There are various accounts of how Pelops emerged victorious. According to some he was a superior charioteer and simply faster than Oenomaus, but a more colorful story is that he managed to win over Oenomaus's blacksmith and persuade him to remove the bronze linchpins from the axles of the king's chariot and replace them with pins made of wax. During the race they heated up and melted. The wheels came off, the chariot broke apart, and Oenomaus was thrown out and killed; Pelops won the race and married Hippodamia. Funeral games were held to mark Oenomaus's burial, and they are said to have given rise to the Olympic Games.

Chariot racing became an official Olympic sport in 680 BC, at least according to Pausanias, who wrote what might be described as a travel guide to Greece in the second century AD, devoting a great deal of space to Olympia, both the visible monuments there and the history bound up with them.[2] It is quite possible that chariot racing had been on the program for some time already, alongside the running, fighting, and throwing events. The impetus to make chariot races a permanent feature must have come from members of the elite, who always did all they could to make a show of their status and their superiority to the common people. They saw chariot racing as an excellent means to this end. At first only four-horse chariots were used, but later two-horse chariots, or *bigae,* were introduced. Special races were occasionally held with chariots pulled by mules or foals, but a shortage of participants meant these events disappeared from the program in the course of the fifth century BC, leaving only the four-horse and two-horse teams.

Based on vase paintings, there is little we can say about Olympic racing chariots other than that they bear a striking resemblance to Egyptian war chariots as depicted in the grave of Tutankhamun, the Egyptian boy king. They were very light, with a floor of interwoven leather straps and a low guard at the front, behind which the driver stood. The two wooden wheels with broad spokes had leather-clad felloes, and they turned around hubs that were fixed to the axle block. From the axle block a long draft pole extended forward, and to it was secured, by a wooden peg, the yoke that went over the horses' necks. In the case of a four-horse chariot with the four horses adjacent, only the two inner horses were directly attached to the yoke. The two outer horses were tied to the yoke by a rein, but they pulled the chariot by means of long traces, which made it easier for them to take the sharp bends at the turns.

Olympic chariot races were not held in the stadium where other events on the program took place but on a field to the southeast. Since hardly any remains of the old Hippodrome have been found, we are reliant on the description by Pausanias. When he refers to the old Hippodrome of Olympia, it is not as a full-fledged sporting arena with tiers of seating, comparable to the racetracks of his own time, but as a large field, prepared for chariot races but without any amenities for spectators. The crowd stood or sat at the two extreme ends of the track, on a high hill to the north and an artificially created bank to the south. Only the umpires and a few high-status visitors had proper seats. The track

A *quadriga* rounding the turning post, on a pan-Athenian amphora of the late fifth century BC. (Photograph by Jastrow)

was some six hundred meters long and two hundred meters wide. The clearly visible turning posts were placed two *stadia*, almost 390 meters, apart.[3]

"Conquer" was the cry to which participants in the Olympia Games entered the fray. Coming in an honorable second counted for nothing, at least as far as the kings, despots, and other aristocrats who signed up to take part in the chariot races were concerned. The tyrants Myron and Cleisthenes of Sicyon, Hiero of Syracuse, and Empedocles of Acragas, ambitious rulers who had done whatever it took to seize power in their cities, felt extremely proud of being able to add their name to the lists of victors. They saw it as confirming their power, and they wasted no opportunity to parade their achievements. Miltiades, Callias, and Alcibiades, fifth-century Athenian politicians who were prominent players in the democratic system of government of their own city, had the same attitude. Since only victory counted, it quite regularly came about that leading aristocrats who owned good horses but thought themselves of insufficient caliber to win races would hire drivers from among the common people. Although their victories were achieved by others, the credit went to the owners of the horses. This meant it was possible for women, who were not permitted to compete in person at the Olympic Games, to win first prizes as owners of victorious *quadrigae.*

It must have been an enthralling spectacle when the chariots shot out of the starting gates, especially from the sixth century onward, when as many as several dozen might take part in a race. Although no figures are given for Olympia, there is written evidence that at the Pythian Games in Delphi in 462 BC forty-one chariots lined up at the start, and so we should assume the numbers in Olympia, too, were large. Forty chariots at a time was probably the exception, but even if only half that number participated, it must have been impossible to make them set off from a straight line perpendicular to the track. The outermost chariots, those on the left in any case, would have been at a considerable disadvantage, needing to leave their lanes almost immediately to head for the ideal course in the center.

The organizers soon came up with a solution. To guarantee the races were as fair as possible and to prevent collisions in the first hundred meters, a broad row of starting gates was placed across the full width of the track, with a separate starting stall for each chariot, held shut by a rope. The result looked rather like the bow of a ship, with the chariots in the center the farthest forward, those at the sides farthest back. Immediately in front of the foremost chariots, in the middle of the track, was a bronze dolphin on top of a pole. A bronze eagle with its wings spread stood on what is described as a small altar, which housed a mechanism for raising the eagle and lowering the dolphin. This was the signal that the ropes across the starting gates could be released in pairs, the outermost ones first, those in the center last. The chariots at the edges of the track raced off while others in the middle were still waiting to start. In contrast to later Roman circuses, there was probably no dividing wall running between the two turning posts, and so the chariots on the left had several hundred meters in which to get themselves over to the right-hand side of the track. An alternative possibility is put forward by John Humphrey in his standard work *Roman Circuses.* Based on Pausanias's description of the starting procedure, he suggests that the track had a wide extension to the right at the starting end and that some of the chariots started off beside the actual track, in

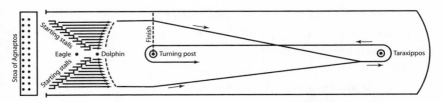

Hypothetical diagram of the start and first lap at the hippodrome in Olympia.

the bow formation described above. In that case none of the chariots would need to cross to the right-hand side by passing between the two posts.[4] They did, however, have to stay in lane until they reached the start of the central barrier.

Only when all the chariots were fully under way did a trumpeter announce with a loud blast that the race proper had begun and the contestants could break for position. Now it was a matter of speed and dexterity, for twelve laps. Each driver knew the risks ahead. He was aware that his opponents would try to drive him off the track and that the crush at the turning posts might prove his downfall. When the trumpeter made himself heard again to signal that the *quadrigae* were on the final straight, the crowd went wild and greeted the winner with thunderous applause.

We have one magnificent report of a chariot race of this kind. It dates from the fifth century BC and comes from Sophocles' tragedy *Electra*. This is not an account of a race that was actually held but a fictional story of a sprint with a tragic outcome during the Pythian Games at Delphi. The fable is told by Orestes' orderly, who tricks Orestes' sister Electra into believing her brother has been killed in a race.

Well now, Orestes, when he was in Delphi,
Had signed up to take part in the sports contests there.
And when the first event, a foot race, was loudly announced,
He stepped forward, admired by all for his fine physique.
As expected, he went on to perform accordingly,
Emerging from the contests the supreme victor.
In short, in my whole life I have never once
Witnessed such a sensational triumph.

In each event that the contest management
Had organized, he carried off the very top prizes.
He was honored as champion by the people
And everywhere his name resounded: Orestes,
From Argos, the son of Agamemnon,
Who was once the general of our proud troops.
So far so good. But what is any man's power,
Or all his abilities, if the heavens thwart him?
Dawn broke on the day that had been reserved
For chariot races. From sunrise onward
Competitors streamed in from all directions.
One was from Sparta, another from Achaea,
Two charioteers were from Libyan lands.
Orestes was named as the fifth competitor,
And he would drive a team of Thessalian horses.
The sixth charioteer was an Aetolian,
His horses brown. Next came a driver
From Magnesia; the eighth was an Aenian,
With his gray stallions, and number nine
Came from Athens, the city of the gods.
Lastly there was a chariot from Boeotia.
They were shown to their places, chosen by lot,
And all the chariots lined up at the start.
Then a loud blast of trumpets sounded,
And they were off. The drivers noisily
Egged on their steeds, their reins pulled taut.
The track was filled with a rattling sound
And the dust flew up, because no driver
Spared the whip or the goad in that tight throng
In his eagerness to overtake the wheels
And pass the snorting teams of his opponents.
Their backs foaming white, the turning wheels too,
They panted onward. Round every lap
Orestes gave rein to the trace horse on the right
While checking the horse on the inner side,
Always cutting close to the turning pillars.
So far none of the drivers had fallen,

But suddenly the Aenian's foals took flight,
Just after the last turn on the sixth lap,
And collided head on with the North African pair.
The crash caused havoc and the whole field
Was like a sea scattered with freshly wrecked driftwood.
The charioteer from Athens saw the incident
In time, and skillfully pulled aside and paused,
While a chaos of smashed chariots could be seen.
Orestes approached, bringing up the rear.
He'd been holding his horses back in the hope
Of a final spurt on the home straight,
But seeing the Athenian was now his one rival,
He gave chase with a deafening crack of the whip.
The horses drew level, neck and neck,
First this one nosing in front, then the other.
They'd completed all the laps but one.
Orestes was still standing straight, poor man, head high . . .
But before the horses came out of the turn
He slackened his left rein and the wheel on that side
Hit the pillar, breaking the axle in two.
He tumbled out of the chariot and was caught
In the tangled reins while his horses raced on
Even though he had fallen, galloping toward
The center of the track. The crowd was shocked
To see him fall and cried out in sympathy.
After such deeds to be struck by such doom!
He banged along the ground, his legs in the air
Till other charioteers managed to hold his horses
And his bloodstained body, unrecognizable
Even to his friends, could be got free.
It was cremated. A small urn of bronze
Contains the ashes of this great hero;
Perhaps a delegation of Phocaeans will come
So that he can be buried in his own native soil.
This, then, is the bad news I bring,
Painful to hear, but for an eyewitness as I am
The greatest disaster I ever experienced.[5]

There must have been many crashes like this. Charioteers regularly lost their lives on the racetrack, to the horror of the spectators. Not that anyone was deterred from watching. People kept coming in large numbers. Nevertheless, and rather surprisingly perhaps, given the spectacular nature of the races, charioteering was not the most popular event on the program. The winners on the racetrack in these years were unable to match the appeal of top boxers and star athletes. They never gained the heroic status of the later charioteers in Rome and Constantinople. This was partly because spectators sat a long way back from the scene of the action, at the short ends of the track, from where they could follow only a small stretch of each race properly. Another factor was no doubt that "ordinary" spectators, those who were not members of the elite, found it hard to identify with their charioteering lords and masters to whom they were obliged to pay so much respect in daily life. To them the environment of the track seemed remote. Chariot races in Olympia and Delphi were always an elitist affair.

Etruria

By the eighth century BC, when Homer wrote his chariot-racing story, equestrian sports were starting to become a familiar pursuit in what is now Italy. They had probably been introduced by Greek colonizers who organized horseracing and charioteering in the cities they founded in the south of the peninsula, as their ancestors had done in Greece. Since no remains of arenas have been found, it seems that here, too, the races took place on stretches of ground naturally suited to the purpose.

Whether the Etruscans, who inhabited a region corresponding roughly to modern-day Tuscany, adopted chariot racing directly from the Greeks is hard to say. They probably organized their races at a relatively late stage, long after the arrival of the Greeks in the Italian peninsula and after they had been enjoying horseracing as entertainment for some time. Depictions in wall paintings, on terracotta tablets, and on vases, which show unsaddled horses being ridden by jockeys holding whips, are convincing evidence that horseracing was popular by the seventh century BC. The earliest pictures of chariots, in frescoes found in burial chambers, date from the sixth century BC, and so the

Etruscans probably encountered chariot racing around that time and not before.

The oldest image ever found of teams of horses, a wall painting in the Tomba della Olimpiadi dating from 530–520 BC, shows a race between *bigae*. The four participants with their two-horse teams are racing toward the turning post. Three are engaged in a fierce contest; the fourth will not finish the race, since one of his horses is lying on its back and the other is rearing up, throwing him out of his chariot. In these as in other depictions there is no sign of permanent facilities. An early fifth-century relief from Chiusi further supports the assumption that races were held in natural settings. It shows a race between three chariots, in this case *trigae*, in other words pulled by teams of three horses, with trees behind them that function not just as a natural backdrop but as the dividing "wall" between the two turning points. The route had to be marked out afresh every time, and low benches were brought in to provide spectators with a modicum of comfort. In a painting from the Tomba delle Bighe that dates from the late sixth or early fifth century BC, Etruscan men and women are shown in a primitive grandstand, little more than a slightly elevated bench covered by a sun shade of some kind. It would not accommodate a large crowd. Notably, no four-horse chariots are shown in any of these pictures, which seems to indicate that the Etruscans initially held races only with *bigae* and *trigae*, rather than *quadrigae*.

The Etruscan charioteers remain anonymous with one exception: Ratumenna of Veii.[6] His name has come down to us in connection with an extraordinary event surrounding Tarquinius Superbus, the last king of Rome, a man of Etruscan descent. Tarquinius had commissioned artists from Veii to make a terracotta *quadriga*, which was to be placed on the central ridge piece of the Temple of Jupiter Optimus Maximus on the Capitol. When the terracotta chariot was baked in the oven, it swelled enormously, and this was interpreted as a sign that whoever came into possession of it would enjoy great power. As a result, the residents of Veii refused to surrender their *quadriga* to the Romans. They felt they had a right to refuse, since Tarquinius Superbus, who had commissioned the work, had meanwhile been banished from Rome. Before long it was time for chariot races to be held in Veii. Ratumenna won, but after crossing the finishing line he did something very strange: he rode on all the way to Rome, turning around only on reaching a gate near the Capitol. The people of Veii saw this as a sign of the might of the Romans and decided to hand over the terracotta chariot to Rome after all. It was placed in the Temple of Jupiter. The gate at which Ratumenna had turned back was named after him. Nothing more is known about this charioteer, but several prominent Etruscan families bore the name Ratumenna, and so it is quite plausible that he was a member of the aristocracy and that the contestants he was up against had similar backgrounds.

Rome

According to the oldest tradition, chronicled by Livy in book 1 of his *History of Rome*, Romulus, the first king of Rome, introduced horse-racing shortly after the city was founded in 753 BC. The races were held in the long valley where a little river called the Murcia flows between the Aventine and Palatine hills. Romulus is said to have organized chariot racing there before long as well. He simply had the valley closed off and personally arranged for chariots and drivers to meet there.

The first occasion on which a racetrack came to public attention to any significant degree was an event known as the Rape of the Sabines. Romulus had foreseen for some time that the Romans would inevitably start to run low on wives, and he feared for the survival of the Roman people as a result. So he thought of a trick. He organized chariot races and invited the Sabines and their daughters. While they were relaxing and watching the races, Roman soldiers suddenly appeared, grabbed the girls, and dragged them off.[7] The fact that Romulus specifically chose the racetrack for this operation suggests that chariot racing appealed to large numbers of people from the earliest times in Rome—and not just to the Romans but to their neighbors as well.

In about 600 BC one of Romulus's successors, Tarquinius Priscus—as tradition would have it, the fifth king of Rome—took the first step toward creating a proper racetrack. He had returned rich with booty from a successful war against the Latins and felt this triumph should be celebrated annually with magnificent games in an appropriate setting. According to Livy, it was then that Tarquinius initiated the building of what was to become the Circus Maximus.[8] He had special seats made for the senators and knights, set four meters or so above the ground on stone bases. From there they watched a program of games that included, along with athletics and boxing matches, horseracing and charioteering. This adaptation of the valley between the Aventine and Palatine hills meant a slow but inexorable turning away from the Etruscan style of chariot racing, since from this point on the races in Rome took place at a real racetrack with seating that did not need to be set up and taken down each time.

These early chariot races were held not simply because a king, or later a republican magistrate, felt like it but in conjunction with special events—a great victory, the triumphal march of a general, or a tribute to one of the gods—and they were components of larger festivals. Romulus himself is said to have set the pattern at his own equestrian festival, called Consualia after the god Consus, a figure parallel to Neptune, the god of the sea and of horses. These events were on a small scale at first, but in time they grew to become a festival held annually on two fixed dates: 21 August and 15 December. Later a second festival was added, the Equirria, held every year on 27 February and 14 March in honor of Mars, the god of war. By the end of the royal era, in roughly 509 BC, chariot racing was the main event on the program at both festivals.

In the five centuries of the republic, chariot races increased in popularity at the expense of other equestrian events. Horseracing remained on the program in the Circus Maximus, but mainly as an accompaniment to the charioteering. Most riders performed as acrobats rather than as proper jockeys, entering the arena with two horses and jumping from one to the other during a race, or working through a series of acrobatic stunts. The growing enthusiasm for chariot racing received a significant boost in the fourth century AD with the expansion of the festival calendar to include a number of sporting events lasting several days, the *ludi*. These were held in honor of specific deities and financed by the state. The oldest were the *ludi Romani*. Livy is the first to mention them, in describing events of the year 366 BC.[9] He says the games had been instigated by the Etruscan king, Tarquinius Superbus, in honor of Jupiter, Juno, and Minerva, to celebrate the anniversary of the inauguration of the Temple of Jupiter on the Capitol on 13 September.

Eventually these *ludi* grew into a festival lasting a fortnight, from 5 to 19 September, with two permanent features: plays and chariot races. More days were set aside for theatrical performances than for charioteering simply because the latter was far more expensive to stage.

In the centuries that followed, many more fixed dates for *ludi* were added to the Roman calendar. The *ludi plebei* in honor of Jupiter were introduced at the beginning of the Second Punic War in 216 BC. They were held every year between 4 and 17 November, with the final three days reserved for chariot races. The *ludi Apollinares* in honor of Apollo were introduced eight years later, in 208 BC, and were always held between 6 and 13 July, with chariot racing on the last two days. Then from 191 BC onward there were the *ludi Megalenses*, held from 4 to 10 April in honor of Cybele, the mother goddess from Phrygia, with one day, the last, entirely devoted to chariot racing. The month of April might in fact be described as a festival month, since from 12 to 19 April the *ludi Cereales* were held, for Ceres, the goddess of fertility, again with one day for chariot racing. Finally, on 27 April the *ludi Florales* began, games for the goddess Flora, which lasted until 3 May. They too featured chariot racing on the final day.

This growth in the number of days on which chariot races were held is closely connected with the changing makeup of the population. In the fifth and fourth centuries BC, Rome grew rapidly, becoming a full-fledged metropolis that was hugely attractive to newcomers. People came to the city from all over the Italian peninsula to make it their permanent home. In the second century BC and thereafter, Rome underwent truly spectacular growth with the arrival of countless foreigners, people from conquered provinces who settled in the city either voluntarily or by order of their new masters. In 218 BC, on the eve of the Second Punic War, Rome had around 125,000 inhabitants, but by 133 BC, when Tiberius Gracchus launched his land reform program, there were already well over 300,000. Most newcomers were not well off; in fact the same was true of the vast majority of the native population, and they were keen to find cheap entertainment in the metropolis. Along with popular theater, athletics, boxing matches, and huge hunting shows with wild beasts (gladiatorial combat was not yet an established form of popular entertainment), chariot races held great appeal, probably partly because people had been familiar with them even before they came to Rome.

The authorities capitalized on this growing enthusiasm. Tiers of seating were built all around the arena and the capacity of the circus gradually increased. Spectators were no longer distant observers; they felt they were part of things, and they could now identify with the charioteers, who were no longer exclusively the sons of senators or knights but often had nonaristocratic backgrounds (see chapter 4). The distinction between the common people and the aristocracy was still obvious from the seating arrangements. Ordinary spectators sat high on the slopes of the Aventine and Palatine hills on the long sides of the Circus Maximus, separated from the senators and knights, who followed the races from seats close to the track

In the last century of the republic two new *ludi* were added. Sulla and Caesar, both dictators, established sporting festivals to commemorate their own achievements. This signified an uncoupling of the traditional link between games and ancient deities. The *ludi victoriae Sullanae*, established by Sulla in 82 BC to celebrate his victory over the Italians, were associated with Victoria, the goddess of victory, who had supported Sulla, but everyone knew they were primarily intended to honor Sulla himself, who liked to be called "restorer of the Roman republic" and "protector and benefactor of the Roman people." The games lasted for five days, between 26 October and 1 November, with one day, the last, reserved for chariot races. Caesar followed Sulla's example and established games of the same kind, the *ludi victoriae Caesaris*, to be held annually between 20 and 30 July. On three of the ten days, chariot races were held. The decision by these two dictators to organize games in their own honor had far-reaching consequences. By taking their sporting festivals out of the traditional religious context, they made way for others to do the same. This laid the basis for the circus games of the imperial era, which were no longer necessarily associated with religious festivities.[10]

The Circus Maximus

Rome conquered the known world in the final two centuries of the republican era and went on to build an immense empire out of a loose collection of provinces. After the republic came to an end in 27 BC and Emperor Augustus founded an absolutist dynasty, he and his successors were keen to convince Rome's subjects that their welfare was safe in their hands. All over the empire they organized major festivals with gladiator fights, stage shows, and chariot races. Charioteering became immensely popular, and local rulers made every effort to lay out suitable circuses within their own city boundaries. From Caesarea in Judea to Santiago do Cacém in Portugal, drivers and horses from all across the empire could perform on dedicated racetracks. Some were beautifully designed, but however much artistry went into them, they faded to insignificance beside the Circus Maximus, which stood, vast and breathtaking, in the center of Rome, a short distance from the Forum Romanum. At first it was not called the Circus Maximus but simply the Circus. After all, it was the only one, and initially it was no more than a field with two turning posts. From the second century BC the Circus Maximus became the stuff of legend, with a fabulous track and high tiers of seating that could eventually accommodate 150,000 spectators.

Anyone standing on the ruins of Domitian's Palace on the Palatine Hill today and tracing the course of the racetrack will see nothing besides the remains of a wall near the Piazza di Porta Capena and the vague outline of the former circus. The rest has gone, prey to the forces of nature, to devastating earthquakes, but perhaps more than anything to rapacious theft over the centuries. Between the early Middle Ages and the nineteenth century the tiers of seating and the wall that separated the two sides of the track were comprehensively demolished. All that now remains is a long, empty green field, surrounded by hills, with the imperial palaces in the background. Nevertheless, even that bare void is impressive.

History

The early history of the Circus Maximus is all but lost to us. There are no ruins left to reveal any details, and the literary legacy is limited to a few remarks by Livy in which he says that Romulus and Tarquinius Priscus organized horseracing there and that Tarquinius turned a stretch of level ground into something that started to look like a real circus. In the late sixth century the last of the kings, Tarquinius Superbus, is said to have expanded the crowd capacity further with permanent stands and to have roofed over some of the seating. It is more than possible, however, that in Livy's imprecise reporting (and that of Dionysius of Halicarnassus) the achievements of the two Tarquinii have became muddled up together and alterations said to have been made by Tarquinius Superbus should really be credited to Tarquinius Priscus.

The infrastructure of the Circus Maximus was repeatedly adapted and improved from the fifth century BC onward, sometimes in the public interest because the games were attracting more and more people, sometimes for the convenience of powerful, influential Romans, as was undoubtedly the case in 494 BC when the dictator Marcus Valerius Maximus and his family began sitting separately from everyone else on a platform of their own.[1] We then hear very little about improvements, adjustments, restoration, or expansion for almost two centuries. The silence is broken by Livy's statement that in 328 BC starting gates (*carceres*) were built, probably of wood.[2] It seems the organizers wanted to make chariot racing more professional and the first requirement was an equitable starting procedure. Until then they had probably used a taut rope, with the chariots lined up behind it, but that was no longer good enough. In the previous few decades the number of participants in each race had grown, and with it the number of false starts.

Whether any significant changes took place in the hundred years that followed is impossible to say. We have no written evidence. It seems there were developments of some kind, since in the third century BC a road was laid from the Forum Boarium (the cattle market) to the Temple of Venus Obsequens, passing close to the Circus Maximus, and we can assume it was intended among other things to help the thousands of visitors who came to watch a day's chariot racing at the Circus Maximus to get there more quickly.

In the second century BC the circus was further refined and decorated. In 196 BC Gaius Stertinus erected a triumphal arch on the outside wall, with gilded statues on top. A short time later the starting gates were improved, permanent turning posts (*metae*) were installed, and a system was invented that used the lowering of stone eggs to indicate how many laps had been completed.

Adjustments were made with the aim of protecting the lowest rows of seating from aggressive wild beasts on the track. It became necessary to build a perimeter wall after the games held by Fulvius Nobilior in 186 BC, when a new event was introduced: the *venationes*, the hunting of wild animals. Lions and tigers were chased and killed in the first of a long series of hunting events in the Circus Maximus, which continued there even after the opening of the Colosseum in AD 80.

Julius Caesar understood that the Circus Maximus was more than simply a place where the populace was entertained. He realized that you needed to give the townsfolk a voice, cut off as they were from political influence—not a voice with any political weight, but the opportunity to make a noise that would bring out into the open what was on ordinary people's minds. Nowhere was more suitable for such a purpose than the Circus Maximus. Caesar lengthened it at both ends, increasing the capacity to more than 150,000. He had a canal dug around the racetrack in front of the stands to give visitors more protection against wild animals that, when cornered, might leap furiously toward them, and stone seats were installed close to the water's edge.[3]

Some of Caesar's alterations were destroyed in a fire that raged through the circus and surrounding area in 31 BC, but Emperor Augustus rebuilt everything that had been lost and came up with further innovations. The author Dionysius of Halicarnassus witnessed the rebuilding in person. In the twenty years and more that he spent in Rome between 31 and 8 BC, he watched the Circus Maximus gain a truly impressive appearance, and he writes that the stands now stretched all around the racetrack, with the exception of the short side behind the starting gates. The lowest seats were made of stone and reserved for senators and knights; above them were stands with wooden seating for the common folk.

During the reigns of Claudius (AD 41–54) and Nero (54–68) further alterations were carried out. After the circus caught fire again, Claudius had the wooden pens behind the starting line replaced with starting stalls made of stone. At the same time he had gilded posts set up to mark the finish.[4] It fell to Nero to respond when the huge conflagration that engulfed a large part of Rome in AD 64 substantially destroyed the circus. We do not know how long the rebuilding took, but it is safe to assume that Nero, a fervent enthusiast for horseracing and charioteering, made sure the work was carried out with all possible speed.

Under Titus (79–81) the outer wall of the Circus Maximus acquired a monument visible a considerable distance away: a tall triumphal arch for the emperor on the short eastern side (not to be confused with the famous Arch of Titus to the south of the Forum Romanum). By erecting it the Senate and the people of Rome intended to portray their vision of Titus as the guardian of Roman imperial ideology. Nothing remains of the arch other than the text of the inscription on it, which tells us the immediate reason why it was built: "With the guidance of his father and under his auspices, he subdued the Jewish people and destroyed the city of Jerusalem, which all generals and kings of other people before him had either attacked without success or left entirely untried."[5] More important perhaps, the arch was erected precisely at the spot where the controversial Nero had demolished part of the entrance in order to create more space for him to drive through triumphantly in an awe-inspiring battle chariot. The building of an arch at that point was intended to give spectators a reassuring sense that a definitive break had been made with the past.

The threat of fire never went away. Small blazes could be quickly doused; major conflagrations forced emperors to rebuild from scratch. During Domitian's reign (81–96) both the long sides were destroyed. Domitian arranged for the restoration to begin but was unable to see it completed before his untimely death. Trajan, who came to power two years later, finished the job. Instead of merely repairing the damage, he gave the Circus Maximus a look and a decor that were talked about all across the Roman Empire. In AD 100 Pliny the Younger, in an oration in which he extolled all Trajan's achievements in turn, wrote about the reconstruction work the new emperor had set in train:

> At another place again the immeasurable facade of the Circus Maximus rivals the most beautiful temples, a suitable space for a people that has subdued the whole world, as much worth seeing in its own right as the contests that will be held there. The beauty of the structure is admirable, and no less so the way in which emperor and people sit next to each other without distinction. The entire length of the Circus offers one and the same view, uninterrupted, without partitions. As a spectator the emperor does not have a loge to himself alone, any more than he has a show staged for himself alone. So all your fellow citizens in turn will be able to see you. They will not be allocated the emperor's loge but they will see the emperor out there in public, surrounded by his people, the people to whom you have given five thousand additional seats.[6]

The Circus Maximus was now a large stone building on three levels, with an arched structure on the ground floor and small pillars on the floors above. Later emperors brought about further changes, but none of a kind that would alter the circus substantially or make it look significantly different. Often they were a direct response by the emperor to a calamity that had struck the circus. Emperor Antoninus Pius (138–61) had to set repairs in train after a supporting pillar high up in the circus became overstressed and gave way, causing some of the higher tiers of seating to collapse. There are references to 1,121 fatalities.[7] Unforced alterations were brought about by Emperor Caracalla (211–17). He was an unpredictable and unpleasant character, but he gave a lot of thought to large-scale building projects, as evidenced to this day by the baths named after him. In 213 he widened the gates of the starting stalls, probably to give the spectators a better view of the chariots as they started off.[8] In the late third century Emperor Diocletian was forced to take decisive action after a major disaster. The wall of the highest stands collapsed over a considerable length, taking thirteen thousand people with it as it fell.[9] Repairs had to be carried out speedily, since Rome's unstable political climate at the time meant the city could not be left for long without chariot races.

Constantine, who became the sole ruler of the western part of the Roman Empire in 312, both renovated and further ornamented the Circus Maximus. He concentrated on the *spina* in particular, the dividing wall at the center of the arena that had always been richly decorated. Constantine's embellishments arose not so much from a spontaneous desire to make the Circus yet more attractive as from political considerations. His defeated rival Maxentius had held power in Rome for six years, time enough to arrange for the building of a circus of his own on the Via Appia, called the Circus Maxentius. One of Constantine's first priorities after his victory over his rival was to negate everything the previous emperor had done. To reduce the prestige of the Circus Maxentius, he ensured that the new decor at the Circus Maximus was especially elaborate. Expansion of the spectator capacity by an unknown number of seats was part of his strategy of showing the public that with him as emperor the people's interests would be catered to. Constantine's successors likewise were concerned with the interior of the Circus Maximus. The obelisk added to the *spina* in 357 by Constantius II is tangible proof that later emperors of antiquity, too, were prepared to make considerable efforts to have their name associated with the Circus Maximus.

Chariot racing went through one final revival in the early fifth century. Competition from gladiator shows in the Colosseum was no longer a factor, since the Christian emperors had ceased to support that particular form of spectacle. Hunting shows and chariot races continued into the sixth century, but as time went on, they were organized less often. The last hunting show in the Circus Maximus was held in 523, the last chariot race in 549 (see chapter 10). The Circus Maximus was left as a magnificent monument to a glorious past, and eventually merely an empty patch of ground.

Features

Under Trajan (98–117) the Circus Maximus had grown to vast proportions. The three other famous monumental buildings in Rome were small in comparison. The circus dwarfed the Theater of Marcellus, Rome's largest theater, with a capacity of 25,000, while the Stadium of Domitian—of which the outlines of the athletics track, more than 200 meters long, can still be traced today on the Piazza Navona—fell even further short of the capacity of the Circus Maximus, since it could seat only 20,000. The Colosseum had room for more than 50,000 spectators, making it by far the largest of the three, but in surface area it was fairly modest compared with the Circus Maximus. This seems an audacious remark, since it is difficult for anyone walking around the astonishing Colosseum to imagine that the Circus Maximus was roughly three times the size. The Colosseum is by any standards highly impressive, with a circumference of 527 meters and notional axes of 188 and 156 meters. Its arena, measuring more than 80 by 54 meters, has a surface area of over 4,000 square meters, and the imposing outer facade on four levels stretches to a height of 52 meters. All of this explains why the Colosseum draws hundreds of thousands of tourists a year as a prime example of Roman monumental architecture.

All the same, the proportions of the Circus Maximus were of a quite different order. There is not enough left of the building to permit an accurate calculation of its measurements. We have only the reports written by authors of antiquity to go on, along with information from other, better-preserved racetracks. According to Dionysius of Halicarnassus, the Circus Maximus, measured from its exterior walls, was three and a half *stadia* long, or 620–660 meters, and four *plethra* (some 120 meters) wide.[10] The length of a row of seating around the two long sides and one short side was 4,800 Greek feet, or 1,400–1,500 meters, and the total crowd capacity was 150,000. These figures are supported, approximately at least, by archaeological work at the site. The length is at the low end of Dionysius's estimate, 620 meters, the width a little greater at 140–150 meters. His report that the benches for spectators ran all around the circus is taken perfectly seriously. Based on research carried out at other circuses, archaeologists assume the benches were stepped back, running the full length and breadth of the circus, each of them stretching for more than 1,400 meters. Each individual seat was 40 centimeters wide and 50 deep, with a height of no more than 33 centimeters.

If this is accurate, then a single row would have provided room for around 3,500 spectators, although given that the benches were interrupted in many places by steps, a more realistic assumption would be 3,000 people per row. The distance between the lowest and the highest

Model of the Circus Maximus. (Photograph by Pradigue)

bench was around 35 meters, which would mean there were 70 tiers of seating in total. Those 35 meters would have been reduced to some extent by aisles between the different zones and by the interior walls, but if we subtract 10 meters to take account of this, 25 meters remain, enough for 50 rows. This gives a total of 150,000 visitors, an enormous number, although low in comparison with the 250,000 spectators Pliny the Elder writes about[11] and far lower than the huge figures of 385,000 and 485,000 that were often cited later in antiquity.[12]

The way the seats were allocated reflects the hierarchy within Roman society. The senators and knights had the best seats, down in the front rows, just high enough to see over the *spina*. They were strictly separated from the ordinary people above them, who sat on the tens of thousands of seats made available cheaply or free of charge by the emperor or wealthy senators. In contrast to the seating arrangements

View from the racetrack of the gates leading to the upper aisles and the lower sections of the stands. The remains of the wall around the higher tiers of seating are also visible. (Photograph by Kalajoki)

at the Colosseum, men and women sat together. The poet Ovid felt this was reason enough in itself for a visit to the Circus Maximus. He shared his feelings with his readers, making several comments in passing that indicate how busy it was in the stands:

> But go to the racetrack, too, with the topnotch horses.
> There, in the packed-out Circus, lies your chance:
> No need to make signs with your fingers to tell your secrets
> Nor to wait for a clandestine message back from her.
> You can sit up close to your lady, there's nothing to stop you,
> And press against her wherever you get the chance,
> In fact you've no option but to press close, that's the rule of the Circus,
> You have to touch your neighbor whether you want to or not.
> You can strike up a general conversation that way too,

Casually, because a polite chat's the best way to start things off.
First ask with interest which horses are competing,
And make sure you choose the one she favors, no matter which.
And when the procession of ivory gods goes by,
Clap for all you're worth for Venus especially.
Perhaps some sand will be thrown onto your girlfriend's clothing.
Wipe it away with your fingers, and if there is none
Then wipe away anyhow as if something were there.
Or if her garments trail too close to the ground,
Helpfully lift them out of the dust for her,
At which point, as a reward, if she allows it,
You might catch a passing glimpse of her legs beneath.
You should also keep an eye on the man behind you,
To make sure he doesn't press her soft back with his knee.
It's worthwhile too—these flighty ladies are swayed by almost anything—
To adjust her cushion with a dexterous touch,
Or create a bit of a breeze with a light fan,
Or set a small stool beneath her tender feet.[13]

People visiting the Circus Maximus for the first time must have been stunned by the sight that greeted them when, stepping into the stands through one of the many entrances from steps on the outside of the massive arches, they took it all in. The endlessly long tiers of seating, the racetrack with the richly decorated *spina*, the starting stalls—it must have made a momentous impression. First-time visitors must have felt small and insignificant in that extraordinary atmosphere, in that environment, amid the noise produced by so many spectators.

The social hierarchy was immediately clear to them. They could see exactly where the greatest authority lay. In the middle of the seating across from the finishing line was the *pulvinar*, the emperor's loge, at one time a simple platform but under Augustus rebuilt as a small sanctuary, from where the emperor and his family would have a good view of the racetrack as they sat in their seats or reclined on couches. By sitting here, the emperor was reinforcing his high status. Wayward emperors who failed to take the custom seriously enough and rarely showed their faces at the circus found their absence counted against them. Domitian, who was in the habit of watching the chariot races from his palace on the Palatine, discovered how true this was. The people were deeply offended by his arrogant attitude and repeatedly made their dissatisfaction clear by whistling and jeering. In contrast, people greatly appreciated the occasions on which an emperor acted in a rather more "democratic" manner by leaving his loge and mingling with ordinary spectators. Trajan is said to have shown he was an emperor of the people by taking a seat among them. Directly across from the emperor, on the other side of the track, precisely in line with the finish, the umpires sat in the clearly identifiable seats reserved for them.

The racetrack itself was between 550 and 580 meters long and a little more than 80 meters wide, which gave it a total surface area of over 44,000 square meters, twelve times the size of the arena in the Colosseum. The ground was covered with fine, high-quality sand, of a grade that would facilitate speed. It had to be capable of absorbing water quickly in the rain and yet not producing too much dust in dry weather. The latter will have been almost impossible to achieve, as the makers of the film *Ben-Hur* discovered for themselves (see chapter 11). The sand was probably replaced regularly, or topped up, and various lines were drawn on it in lime or later in chalk. A set of lanes ran from the starting stalls to just short of the closer of the two turning posts, a distance of around 160 meters. This was to prevent the drivers breaking for position too early and taking the shortest route to the center, to the inside part of the right-hand side of the track. A line running at right angles to the lanes where they reached the first turning post indicated that from that point on the drivers were free to choose their ideal route. Directly in front of the umpires was another line: the finish.

The starting stalls (*carceres*) were quite ingenious. Unfortunately there are no known remains of the artfully constructed starting gates at the Circus Maximus, but excavations at the best-preserved arena of all, at Leptis Magna (Libya), along with observations in ancient literature, make clear that the Romans did all they could to ensure the starting procedure was as fair as possible. They had learned from the Greeks that the chariots could not simply be positioned behind a line to set off side by side. The starting system at Olympia, with its arrangement of chariots like the bow of a ship, had proved a workable solution, yet the Romans did not adopt this procedure, probably because in the Circus

Maximus it was unusual for more than twelve *quadrigae* to compete in a single race. The starting stalls were arranged in a pattern that had been worked out with great precision, covering the full width of the track and curving back at the center, with those on the left a little farther forward than those on the right. The curve and the distance were calculated such that the chariots to the left of the center were closest to the *spina*.

The arena had two main gates. The chariots came in through the gate on the western side of the Circus Maximus and made their way to their starting stalls, which were allocated by drawing lots. Each stall was about six meters wide and had two broad doors, held shut under tension by sinews twisted together until they were taut. On the outside they were locked with firm bolts. When the starting signal was given, the bolts were pulled back by means of ropes that came together on a platform above the starting stalls, where they were joined, so that all the gates were unlocked simultaneously. A catapult mechanism opened the latches, releasing the tension in the sinews, whereupon the doors flew open with a bang.[14] At the far end of the circus was another gate, the Porta Libitinaria, through which charioteers who had been forced to abandon the race or were seriously injured left the arena, sometimes carried out on stretchers.

In the middle of the course was the *spina*, 340 meters long. Originally it was nothing more than a stone barrier between the two sides of the track, but under Trajan it became a double wall enclosing a deep pool of water, which has led some experts to speak not of a *spina* but of a *euripus*, or canal. At the ends of the wall stood the *metae*, the turning points. The earliest version of these looked rather like the wooden tree trunks used in Homeric times, but from the early first century AD they consisted of three conical pillars on a firm base, clearly recognizable by the drivers and spectators as marking the turns. The solid cones were firmly anchored, so that they stayed upright if one or more chariots crashed into them. Instead of running straight from one end of the track to the other, the wall was probably set at a slight angle, to make turning easier. Where the chariots began to steer into the turn the track narrowed a little, and on the other side it was rather wider, so that the charioteers did not have to rein in their horses too much as they swung wide coming out of the bend.

The attention of visitors was immediately drawn to the ornamentation on the *spina* and the statues on top of it. The obelisk of the Egyptian pharaoh Ramses II, which Augustus had ordered to be brought to Rome in 10 BC from Heliopolis, the center of the sun cult, was the most eye-catching of all. It was nearly twenty-four meters high, on a plinth of more than three meters. In 1587, when the Circus Maximus was definitively dismantled, Pope Sixtus V transferred the obelisk to the Piazza del Popolo, where it now stands at the center of the oval piazza. In the fourth century, on the initiative of Emperor Constantius II (337–61), another obelisk was added to the *spina*, that of Egyptian pharaoh Thutmose III. Sixtus V removed this obelisk too from the Circus Maximus, erecting it on the square in front of the Basilica of St. John Lateran.

There were several reasons for placing these obelisks high on the *spina*. Their significance was derived in part from the beliefs of the Egyptians, who regarded an obelisk as a connection between the earth and the sun god Re. In Roman eyes the racetrack and everything that went with it was a model of the cosmos in miniature: the obelisk was the sun, the arena the earth, the pools of water inside the double wall the sea, while the four colors of the racing stables stood for the seasons, the twelve starting stalls for the signs of the zodiac, the three cones of each of the *metae* for the *decani* (key days) of an astronomical month, and the twenty-four races for the hours of the day.[15]

The symbols used to indicate the number of laps the competitors had yet to complete were set in a mythological context as well. The seven stones or wooden eggs, lowered one by one, symbolized the twin gods Castor and Pollux, who had hatched from an egg. The eggs were later replaced by dolphins, to emphasize the connection with Neptune, the god not just of the sea but of horses. Each time the chariots finished a lap, one of the seven dolphins would dip down into the water-filled basin between the two walls of the *spina*.

On the *spina*, along with the obelisk or obelisks, were three columns bearing statues of Victoria, goddess of victory, Cybele, goddess of fertility, and the agrarian goddess Seia or Messia. A second statue of Cybele depicted her riding a lion. There must have been a great deal more besides. Various authors talk of a large palm tree, altars, a small temple, and statues of other, unspecified goddesses. Outstanding charioteers with more than a thousand victories to their name hoped they might

The obelisk erected on the *spina* at the Circus Maximus by Constantius II, which now stands in front of the Basilica of St. John Lateran. (Photograph by Matthias Kabel)

be honored with a statue on the *spina* after their death. For spectators the *spina* represented a link between the cosmos and the reality of the racetrack.[16]

Other Racetracks in Rome

Surprisingly perhaps, with the Circus Maximus in the center of the city, there were other racetracks in Rome. It is yet another indication of just how popular chariot racing was and how eagerly powerful figures capitalized on it by having circuses built that would always be associated with their name. The second oldest in Rome was the Circus Flaminius, lying to the northwest of the Circus Maximus between the sites where the Theater of Pompey and the Theater of Marcellus would later stand (see map 2). The two circuses had little in common. The one built by Gaius Flaminius in 220 BC was oval in shape and less suitable for chariot racing than the Circus Maximus. It was more like a multifunctional theater in which mass gatherings of ordinary people or soldiers could be held. Since no remains of a *spina* or proper seating tiers have been found, it seems the Circus Flaminius was used for chariot races only on special occasions. We know that Augustus used it for other forms of spectacle. In 2 BC he had the Circus Flaminius flooded, probably by digging a pool in the center of the arena, and brought in thirty-six crocodiles.[17] After satisfying the curiosity of the crowd they were slaughtered.

Slightly better known is the Circus of Gaius (Caligula) and Nero, also known as the Circus Vaticanus, since it was laid out where St. Peter's and the famous square in front of it are now. At 560 meters long and 80 meters wide, the track was only marginally smaller than that of the Circus Maximus. The starting stalls were at the edge of the present square, where the Via della Conciliazione interrupts the colonnades. Caligula, a great fan of chariot racing and an emperor with boundless delusions of grandeur, initiated its construction. He had in mind a private racetrack where he would be able to watch the art of charioteering as demonstrated by the drivers of the Greens, his favorites. He wanted his circus to rival the Circus Maximus, and to convince the Romans it was of an equal caliber he had a huge obelisk brought from Egypt on a ship specially built for the purpose. It was the largest obelisk ever to decorate the *spina* of a circus, compared with which even the obelisk in the Circus Maximus was small. It now stands in all its glory in the middle of St. Peter's Square, not far from the spot it occupied in Caligula's day.

Caligula did not live to see his circus completed. He was deposed before it was ready for use. His successor, Claudius, allowed the work to continue and held chariot races there several times, as did Nero, who came after him. This circus never rivaled the Circus Maximus, however. Vespasian, who did his best to eliminate everything reminiscent of Nero's misrule, turned it into a park.

A third circus, the Circus Varianus, was built in the early third century on the initiative of two emperors with a great love of chariot racing and a taste for extremes: Caracalla (211–17) and Heliogabalus (218–22). Their arena was part of a palace complex called Sessorium, not far from where the Basilica di Santa Croce in Gerusalemme now stands. It was remarkable for its vast exterior dimensions, with a width of 115–125 meters and a length of roughly 565 meters, and here too a large obelisk stood in the middle of the *spina*. The circus served as a racetrack for only fifty years. In the course of the third century pressure on the empire's borders increased, and there was a fear that invaders might attack the imperial capital, and so about AD 270 Emperor Aurelian had a defensive wall built around the city. This Aurelian Wall ran straight across the Circus Varianus. A small stretch of the racetrack, a little over a hundred meters, came to lie inside the wall, the rest outside. Virtually nothing is left. The outer walls and the *spina* have gone, and only the obelisk, more than nine meters high, still evokes memories of the splendor of Heliogabalus's circus; it was moved to the Palazzo Barberini in 1632, then in 1769 to the Vatican, before being given its current place in the Monte Pincio Park above the Piazza del Popolo in 1822.

The best-preserved circus in Rome lies between the second and third milestones along the Via Appia, as counted from the Forum Romanum. A visitor can form a good general impression here of a late Roman circus, in this case one that formed part of a large palace complex that included a mausoleum. The whole complex was built by Maxentius in the sixth year of his reign, before he was defeated by Constantine at the Milvian Bridge in 312. It is a truly remarkable circus in the sense

One of the tall towers that stood at either end of the starting stalls of the Circus Maxentius. (Photograph by Pascal Reusch)

that the length and breadth of the arena, 503 by 75–79 meters, fell only marginally short of those of the Circus Maximus, but the external measurements are not much bigger, at 520 by 92 meters, which suggests that the spectator capacity was limited to ten thousand at most. Clearly this was never a truly public circus. It was probably used mainly for chariot races held to entertain a carefully selected audience. Apparently this was no reason to make it any more sober in its construction; the remains of the Circus Maxentius—the walls of the stands, the seating, the towers on either side of the starting stalls, and the seats for the umpires—demonstrate that Maxentius's builders paid a great deal of attention to the decor. The showpiece of the *spina*, the obelisk, brought by Emperor Domitian from the Alps this time rather than Egypt, was moved by Pope Innocent X in 1650 to the Piazza Navona, where it now stands on Bernini's Fountain of the Four Rivers.

Racetracks outside Italy

Wherever Roman conquerors took power, they introduced gladiator fights, hunting shows, and chariot races, and almost everywhere these initiatives were warmly welcomed. Governors of the main towns and cities of the empire did not need to think very hard before deciding to build new amphitheaters and racetracks, given that such facilities brought prestige to a municipality, strengthened ties between its population and the emperor, and presented local magistrates with a chance to increase their popularity by contracting top athletes. Impressive racetracks were not confined to regions rich in horses. The authorities elsewhere were keen to avoid falling behind. In the first century AD there was a veritable building boom, with a large number of circuses laid out in North Africa, Spain, Gaul, Palestine, Egypt, and Syria. Some were virtual replicas of the Circus Maximus, others no more than fields with a small amount of seating to accommodate spectators, looking more like the racetracks of ancient Greece.

The best-preserved circus is in Libya, in what was once Leptis Magna. It dates from the second century, when things were going well for the region. Compared with the racetracks in Rome, it is small, at 450 meters long and 70 meters wide, with room for 22,000 spectators, but if there is a circus that illustrates the meticulous way in which the master builders set about their work, then it is this one. The ingeniously constructed starting stalls, the steps up to the tiers of seating, the sensibly proportioned seats, the aisles, and the remains of the *spina* are evidence of great artistry on the part of the designers.

One might think that once a wealthy North African city like this had acquired such a splendid circus, other cities would try to emulate it. There is no truth in this assumption. Remains of racetracks elsewhere in North Africa exhibit a different, more sober building style. The circus laid out a century earlier in Carthage, measuring 500 by 78 meters with a capacity of 40,000, was admittedly larger, but it had none of the ornamentation, luxury, and quality of design exhibited by the circus at Leptis Magna. The same goes for the racetracks in other, smaller towns in the province of Africa Proconsularis: Utica, Thysdrus, and Hadrumetum. But the mere fact that governors of middle-sized towns released funds for the building of large circuses indicates the importance they attached to chariot races.

Impressive racetracks were built in Spain and Portugal, too. They lie scattered right across the Iberian Peninsula, all the way to the west coast. There were arenas in Tarragona, Saguntum, Toledo, Calahorra, Mérida, Italica, and Santiago do Cacém in Portugal. City magistrates knew that by organizing chariot races in honor of the emperor they were improving their prospects of a career in the imperial government. People found them magnificent; in Spain chariot racing was enormously popular. It is no accident that one of Rome's most famous charioteers, Gaius Appuleius Diocles, was a Spaniard, a native of Lusitania.

In Gaul there were arenas at Lyon, Arles, Saintes, and Vienne, but only the circus built in Arles under Emperor Antoninus Pius (138–61) is reasonably well preserved. It was a medium-sized circus, 450 meters long and 80 meters wide. No trace has been found of the other racetracks. They lie buried under the dust of centuries or beneath later buildings. Of the circus in Lyon only a handful of inscriptions referring to chariot races remain, plus an impressive mosaic depicting a race in a circus whose facilities show a striking resemblance to those of the Circus Maximus. Nothing is left of the circus in Vienne other than a fifteen-meter-tall obelisk that once decorated the *spina*.

In Germania there is no evidence of arenas in great cities like Cologne and Mainz, but this is not to say, necessarily, they lacked racetracks of their own. It does seem that chariot races were less popular in Germany. The one German city that we can be absolutely certain had a circus suitable for chariot racing is Trier. A racetrack measuring 440 by 80 meters was built there during the reign of Emperor Constantine in the early fourth century, on top of an earlier track.

If anything, it is even harder to be sure whether Britannia had circuses. Nowhere have remains been found that point to the existence of proper racetracks. If races were held, they probably took place on improvised tracks on the outskirts of cities.

The situation in the eastern part of the Roman Empire was very different. In Egypt, Palestine, and Syria imposing circuses went up, although only after the Roman circus had become a familiar phenomenon in other parts of the empire. The racetracks at Antioch, Caesarea, Antinoopolis, Gerasa, Bostra, and Gortyn were built in the second century AD. In the century that followed, Laodicea, Constantinople (then still called Byzantium), and Tyre acquired circuses that fired the imagination. The circus at Antioch was the largest, with a racetrack of more than 492 by 70–75 meters, surrounded by tiered seating for 80,000 spectators. It was clearly intended as a copy of the Circus Maximus. The smallest was at Gerasa, where the arena was 244 meters long at most and only 51 meters wide.

Remarkably, in Greece and Asia Minor, the heartlands of Hellenic civilization, there was hardly any building activity of this type. Interest in chariot racing had been in decline there since the third century BC, a trend that continued into the early imperial era, although races were still held on the old tracks at Olympia, Delphi, and Nemea.

At the end of the third century AD, Emperor Diocletian moved the center of government from Rome to four new residences: Trier, Milan, Sirmium, and Nicomedia. Each of these four cities was endowed with a large circus. The tetrarchy was not destined to last. After a long-drawn-out struggle for the throne against a number of rivals, Constantine put an end to the system. As his center of government he chose the city he had founded himself, Constantinople, and he ensured it had a racetrack that reflected the glory of the new Rome by transforming its existing circus into the imposing Hippodrome. The palace Constantine built virtually adjoining the Hippodrome illustrates once again how bound up with each other imperial power and chariot races were in this period.

CHAPTER 4

Preparation and Organization

According to the Calendar of Philocalus, a manuscript produced in 354, Rome had 176 registered feast days that year: 102 for theatrical performances, 64 for chariot races, and only 10 for gladiator shows. That so few days were reserved for gladiatorial combat is entirely understandable, since it demanded not just considerable financial investment but long preparation. The transportation of wild animals from all parts of the empire alone called for careful planning. Chariot races were easier to organize. The well-trained horses in the racing stables could be deployed at any time. The magistrates, charged with the task of organizing racing events, made the initial outlay without complaint. They drew on state funding in doing so but paid out of their own pockets as well, since they knew it was a way to enhance their image.

At first the organizers, who in the early republic were mainly *aediles*, the supervisors of public works, looked to the horse-owning aristocracy whenever they needed charioteers. At festivals aristocrats competed against one another with their own horses and at their own expense. It was a matter of honor. Victory reflected well on them and enhanced their prestige. In this early phase their performances are strongly reminiscent of those of the Greek and Etruscan charioteers, but in the fourth century BC change set in. Roman aristocrats still wanted to make their mark in life, but they were increasingly aware that true *laus et gloria* (fame and glory) were to be achieved in successful wars and in politics, not on the racetrack. Their eagerness to train and to compete in the arena declined until they were relatively indifferent to the prospect. It became harder and harder to persuade them to perform, while at the same time the chariot races grew in popularity, and so more charioteers were wanted than ever. The organizers had to look for drivers among other groups in the population, not an easy task given that few people outside the elite of senators and knights were in possession of racing-caliber horses. The aristocracy probably managed to make up the shortfall for a while by contracting drivers from lower social groups and providing them with suitable horses.

In the mid-third century BC, when the supply of both drivers and horses fell far short of demand, the organizers invented a new system that would enable them to sign up sufficient charioteers. Any Roman, whatever his status, could arrange a price for providing horses and drivers for a show. Since wealthy senators were no longer likely to participate, other individuals were given an opportunity to write their asking price on special lists. Wealth in Rome was concentrated mainly in the senatorial class, and few people had sufficient capital to take a financial risk, but by pooling their capital ordinary citizens could meet the requirements for participation, and slowly a setup developed that allowed them to form joint ventures and reach financial agreements. This was the start of the racing stables system. After a while the largest stables grew into tightly run organizations that concentrated on breeding and training horses, experimenting with racing chariots, and instructing drivers. When aristocrats stopped performing as charioteers, circus racing declined in prestige within the elite. Whereas it had once been primarily a competition between prominent Romans in which honor alone was at stake, the racing of four-horse chariots now became a professional activity, engaged in mainly by people of humble origin.

Charioteering received a powerful boost in the second century BC. Conquests across the whole of the Mediterranean region set in motion a tremendous flow of capital in the direction of Rome. The government invested most of the money in prestigious building projects, including the expansion of the Circus Maximus, but chariot racing also profited directly from this "new money." Many magistrates who had brought back substantial booty after serving as generals in the wars of expansion invested a proportion of their newly acquired wealth in the staging of expensive shows. They signed contracts with the directors of the racing stables for the supply of horses and charioteers. Circus games became more than merely entertainments offered on fixed dates; they were now professionally produced spectacles involving high-quality equipment and trained drivers—and considerable prize money.

The general public responded with appreciation, entering into the spirit of the chariot races more than ever and steadily becoming better able to judge what made a good show. The organizers for their part realized that only truly thrilling races would boost their image, so they became more selective, signing up horses and drivers only if they were on a par with the competition. As a result, an intense fight for survival broke out between the stables, ultimately to the detriment of the smaller among them, which ceased to exist, fused with other stables, or were simply taken over.

The Racing Stables

By the end of the first century BC there were four large racing stables, each with its own faithful band of supporters. Referred to as *factiones*, they took their names from the color of their chariots: the Greens (*factio prasina*), the Blues (*factio veneta*), the Reds (*factio russata*), and the Whites (*factio albata*).[1] According to the authors Tertullian (third century) and Isidore of Seville (seventh century), the colors of the factions were clearly connected with the seasons and the elements: green pointed to the spring, the earth, the flowers, and Venus; red meant the summer, fire, and Mars; blue stood for the autumn, the sky, and the waters of the sea; white represented the winter, the air, the west wind, and Jupiter.[2]

The stables of all four *factiones* were on the Campus Martius, less than two kilometers from the Circus Maximus. The Green and Blue stables were the largest, with their own racetracks for training and many accompanying buildings. The Greens' facilities were at the spot where the Palazzo della Cancelleria now stands; the Blues occupied what is now the Piazza Farnese. These were large complexes where dozens of charioteers and hundreds of horses could train in optimal conditions. The bosses of each stable would make sure their drivers had everything they needed, since they knew they could not afford to let their stable lose too often.

The four racing stables were household names and would remain so for centuries, not just in Rome but in all the provincial cities of the empire where the system was copied and later in Constantinople. Remarkably, the divisions between different strata of the population, so characteristic of Roman society, seem to have dissolved within support-ers' groups. Members of the elite and ordinary people could support the same stable. They behaved very much like the fans of today's foot-ball clubs. As long as things were going well, they cheered their favorite drivers, but if victory eluded them, they would be thrown into deep despondency or rage and chant hostile slogans. Sometimes they were unable to keep a grip on themselves and lashed out at rival supporters, and they were also quite likely to turn against the leaders of their own stables, holding them responsible for the defeat of their charioteers.

The supporters had no involvement in the organization of their cho-sen stable. A small management team with a *dominus factionis* at its head, perhaps best described as a president and director, was respon-sible for running everything. This overall boss was selected from the ranks of the *equites*, the Roman knighthood, which had considerable trading interests, and so he knew how to handle money. Some directors brought in enormous sums for their stables, and since they were well aware that without their cooperation no shows of a passable standard could be staged, they often put the organizers of chariot racing events under severe pressure. Usually the organizers gave in and handed over large sums of money to the stables to ensure the races could be held. Sometimes they dug in their heels and refused to pay the full asking price.

Occasionally the emperor was forced to mediate in person. In AD 54, shortly after he took office, Nero had to step in when Aulus Fab-ricius, organizing races on Nero's behalf, refused to concede to the financial demands of the racing stables, which he accused of blackmail. When negotiations broke down, he renounced their services and took a truly radical step. To the horror of the leaders of the stables he ordered that dogs be trained to pull chariots. On the day of the races it became clear that Fabricius was serious. The dogs were brought out onto the track. The Reds and the Whites, the smaller racing stables, gave in at that point and accepted the conditions proposed by the organizers. The Greens and Blues refused to budge, but in the end a generous offer from Nero changed their mind, and the races went ahead.[3]

The racing stables were professional organizations, and their many employees assisted the charioteers in a number of ways. Inscriptions have been found that clearly describe the various specialized functions.[4]

First there were the *conditores* and the *sellarii*, who together with their assistants were responsible for the day-to-day running of the training complex. During the chariot races at the Circus Maximus they ensured that the drivers had everything they needed and would turn up at the starting line well equipped. A crucial task was reserved for the *tentores*, who opened the starting gates at a signal from the official starter, until an improved mechanism made it possible for the starter to open all the gates himself. Great skill was required of a *tentor*, since a poor start meant a long struggle to catch up. The care of the horses was in the hands of the *moratores*, dedicated stable lads who slept with their charges and put them at ease, tending to them until the moment they set off. During the starting procedure they stood in the stalls waiting to release the horses at precisely the right moment. Spread out along the racetrack stood the *sparsores*. It was their job to sprinkle the charioteers and horses with water as they passed. They probably also threw water over the chariot axles, which would rapidly heat up.[5] The *hortatores* had a rather curious task. During the races they rode on horseback between the chariots, keeping drivers from their own stables apprised of how things were going, especially out of sight to their rear. They wore the colors of their stables, and so they were easy for the crowd to identify. Apart from these helpers, who appeared in their own training arenas as well as at the Circus Maximus, there were of course doctors and vets, as well as masseurs who worked behind the scenes to keep both the horses and the charioteers in peak condition.

The Horses

Under normal circumstances there was rarely, if ever, a shortage of horses capable of competing at the highest level, since the bosses of the racing stables knew exactly where in the Roman Empire to look for the best animals. The breeding of horses was a centuries-old tradition in the Mediterranean world, where since time immemorial the possession of beautiful, swift horses had enhanced a person's status. Some owners had even written down their findings in the form of treatises. The best known was by an Athenian, Xenophon (428–354 BC), a writer on many diverse subjects. In his *On Horsemanship* he takes a close look at horse breeding and considers various aspects: the height of the horse, the set of the eyes, typical behaviors, the relationship of trust with grooms and stable lads, daily exercise, care, stabling, and feed.

The Romans inherited the scientific foundation given to horse breeding by the Greeks and developed it further. Writers Pliny the Elder and Columella were not themselves involved in the breeding of horses in the early imperial period, but from their observations it is clear that they were well informed about the standards required to place a horse in the highest category. One remarkable source of information is Pelagonius, a fourth-century vet who wrote at length about the physical characteristics of racehorses and came up with remedies for frequently occurring ailments and injuries. These treatises prove beyond doubt that Roman breeders and the bosses of racing stables knew precisely how to prepare their horses for the demands of the track.

The horses on the racetrack were the largest and fastest of their time. Horse bones found at a number of locations that were once part of the Roman Empire allow us to estimate their height. By our standards they were not very big: 13.5–15.5 hands high (or about 1.35–1.55 meters), some 1.5 hands (15 centimeters) shorter than today's racehorses, which average 16–16.5 hands (roughly 1.60–1.65 meters).[6]

The most famous sources of racehorses were Cappadocia in eastern Turkey, Spain, Sicily, and North Africa, especially a region that is now part of Libya. Top breeders there and elsewhere in the empire were visited by dealers who had been commissioned by the directors of the racing stables to go out in search of the best horses. The trade was widespread, and it provided work for many people; in fact, several grave inscriptions have been found which clearly indicate that horse dealers, instead of working on their own behalf, usually represented a corporation, called a *collegium* or *sodalicitas*. At their disposal were a number of horse transports, known as *hippagogi*. These were sailing ships or galleys with holds that had been adapted to accommodate several dozen horses at a time. In later periods the most famous breeds could, of course, be sourced from stud farms in districts close to Rome.

Horses that had proven their worth in the smaller circuses were regularly brought to Rome by order of a racing stable. Conversely, horses judged not good enough for the Circus Maximus were sold to stables in provincial towns. Although the ancient sources make no mention of it, we can assume that some of the horses in the Circus Maximus were the product of deliberate crossbreeding. Breeders and trainers knew the specific characteristics of horses from different regions, and they must have wanted to introduce those traits into breeds with other outstanding qualities.

If the charioteer inscriptions that mention specific breeds are a fair reflection of reality, we can be virtually certain that horses from North Africa were the most highly prized by the majority of drivers. Teres and Diocles, top charioteers of the early second century, are quite outspoken in their preference for African horses. In an inscription found on one of the walls of the Castel Sant' Angelo, Teres informs us that of the forty-two top horses in his charge, thirty-seven were from North Africa, two from Spain, one from Gaul, and one from Greece. Of the African horses, two were hugely successful: Callidromus achieved more than a hundred victories, while Hilarus managed over a thousand.[7] Diocles was proud to belong to that select group of charioteers who were able to drive the fiery African steeds effectively. It has been claimed that African horses were the forerunners of our Arab thoroughbreds, famous for giving their all on the racetrack, but there is no firm evidence of this.[8]

The horses in the racing stables, almost always young stallions, were subjected to an intensive training program. First they had to get used to the *longe*, a six-meter line with which the trainer walked them in circles and taught them to follow commands and to switch between a walk, a trot, and a gallop. When a horse had mastered the basics, an assessment was made as to the position in which it could best be deployed: as a middle horse under the yoke or as a trace horse on the outside. Once it was comfortable wearing the bridle (tack that consisted of straps around the neck, chest, and belly), the yoke, the draft pole, and the reins, it was put into a team, first with one or two other horses and then, if all went well, a four-horse team. At this point it was subjected to proper endurance, interval, and speed training. Special attention was paid to the starting procedure and the turns, since it was there that the greatest time advantages were to be gained.

There was a danger that horses might be overtaxed during training, and so they were under permanent supervision by vets. Special attention was paid to their hooves; horses were not shod, and their hooves wore down quickly on the hard ground. The vets also kept a close

A charioteer holds his horse by the bridle. (Photograph by Jastrow)

watch on their joints and tendons, which were severely tested in the sharp turns. If necessary, a horse would be taken out of a team and prescribed a period of rest.

Training was not the same for every horse. The horses that raced on the inside of the track practiced mainly tight cornering and changes of pace, while the yoke horses learned to maintain a good speed and horses on the outer or right-hand side were taught to cover more ground in the turns.

Horses had several years' training behind them by the time they were first entered for official races. At least two years old when they were accepted by the racing stables, they were not raced until their fifth year.

Barring an injury that put it out of the running, a horse might be active on the track for ten to fifteen years. Few horses would have raced for so long, but among those that did were the real winners, with many dozens, sometimes even hundreds, of victories to their name.

On a normal circus day there were usually 24 races. Each involved 4, 8, or 12 chariots lining up at the start, on rare occasions 16. If we assume an average of 8 chariots per race, 2 from each stable, in a single day 192 chariots would have been deployed, an average of almost 50 from each racing stable. Of course a chariot could be driven in several of the day's races, and so the actual number needed was far smaller. With the horses that were harnessed to them it was a different story. Most saw action only once on any given day. A few top horses might be entered a second time, in races for extremely high prize money. Assuming that in the vast majority of cases four-horse chariots were raced, only occasionally two- or three-horse chariots (and in very exceptional cases six- to ten-horse teams), we can make a rough estimate of the number of horses required. Multiplying 192 chariots by between three and four gives a total of between 600 and 800 horses, or 150 to 200 per stable. Given that there was a fair likelihood a horse might be put out of action permanently in one of the many collisions at the turns, we can be reasonably certain that all four racing stables would have to absorb the loss of one or more horses by the end of an average race day. To avoid running short, the leaders of each racing stable would have taken the precaution of holding in reserve plenty of horses that were fully prepared to race.

Successful horses were loved by the general public. On the street and in the bars near the Circus Maximus, the precise characteristics of the top horses were the main topic of conversation. Most supporters knew exactly how old their favorite horses were, where they came from, how often they had won, and with which horses and charioteers they raced as a team. Some fans became so obsessed that they could barely be dragged away from the stables and never missed a training session. A few, their enthusiasm bordering on mania, even took the droppings of their favorite horses home with them to check that they had not eaten anything untoward.[9]

Some people felt all this went way too far. The poet Martial had difficulty reconciling himself to the fact that his own fame was as nothing compared with the renown enjoyed by a famous racehorse:

> I am Martial, author of fine verse full of kindly wit,
> Famous throughout the world as a result of it.
> Yet envy me not! I am of course
> Less famous than Adraemon the horse.[10]

More than two centuries later, Christian author John Chrysostom expressed his displeasure at the great popularity of horses and charioteers. He writes with horror that the people of Rome can name top horses but are quite unable to say how many apostles there were.[11]

Many dozens of horse names were immortalized on mosaics and amphorae and in inscriptions. Most reflect one special quality of a horse or call to mind a legendary mythological figure. A snowy gray bore the name Candidus (white), a horse with an eye-catching mane was called Crinitus (curly), a mottled horse was named Maculosus (speckled), and a particularly quick horse might be called Cursor (runner) or Sagitta (arrow). Horses that had notched up many victories were named Polyneices (often conquering) or Palmatus (with many palms of honor). Frequently chosen names from mythology were Pegasus, Castor, Pollux, Achilles, and Ajax. Sometimes a horse would be named for another animal: Leo (the lion), Catta (the cat), or Aquila (the eagle). Some horses were remembered long after their death, while others were inseparable in people's minds from specific charioteers, and a few of the most successful were even buried in the same grave as their regular drivers.

The Chariots

Because no full-sized chariots have survived and there are hardly any detailed descriptions, we are reliant almost entirely on images from frescoes, reliefs, vases, and oil lamps. Several of these are truly captivating and clearly show the specific features of a racing chariot; others are so vague that the constituent parts are almost impossible to make out. In some cases it is not even clear whether the chariot shown is actually a racing chariot or a triumphal chariot of the kind used in the ceremonial processions for Roman generals that were held to mark famous victories. Triumphal chariots were generally of the same basic design but much heavier; they were rather like floats, richly ornamented, differently hitched, and not at all suitable for driving at high speeds.

In addition to pictures we have several scale models of racing chariots. It is impossible to overstate the importance of these. They give us an idea of the relationship between the dimensions of the various components and the weight of the chariot as a whole. Probably the most true to life is a bronze model of a two-horse chariot that was found in the Tiber. It shows unambiguously that racing chariots must have been very light, probably weighing no more than twenty-five to thirty-five kilos. They were constructed out of thin wooden slats or sturdy basketwork, reinforced with leather strapping and brightly painted in the colors of their stables. The width of a chariot axle was around 1.60 meters, the distance between the wheels 1.55 meters, and the floor of the body of the chariot roughly 55 by 60 centimeters. The wheels were no more than 60 centimeters in diameter, with six or eight spokes. The charioteer stood behind a semicircular guard that was about 70 centimeters high. From the chariot a draft pole measuring some 2.30 meters extended upward at a shallow angle, curving toward the end, where a yoke about a meter wide would be fixed. The yoke was secured to the tack worn by the two middle horses (*iugales*) just above the withers. The two outer horses were directly attached to the chariot by traces (*funes*) and were therefore called *funales,* or trace horses. By pulling on the reins or slackening them, a charioteer was able to steer the two outer horses at the tight turns.[12]

The Charioteers

The Romans had two words for charioteer: *auriga* and *agitator*. These were not synonyms but terms consciously chosen to refer to two different categories. A young, inexperienced driver who had yet to learn the trade and who raced in a two-horse chariot was usually referred to as an *auriga*, while an *agitator* was a more experienced colleague who drove almost exclusively in four-horse chariots.

Roman charioteers looked quite different from their Greek prede-

Bronze statue of a charioteer, found in Delphi. It was originally part of a monument that featured a *quadriga*. (Photograph by Gunnar Bach Pedersen)

cessors as we know them from vases and statues. If we compare the famous Greek bronze statue *The Charioteer of Delphi* with a Roman marble sculpture of a charioteer from the second century AD, the differences are immediately obvious. The Greek driver wears a *chiton*, a long robe that would offer no protection at all should his chariot meet with an accident, and around his head he has a hair band. The Etruscans had shortened the *chiton* and given the driver a cap to wear, but Roman charioteers wore truly professional-looking protective clothing that gave them some chance of survival should they be thrown out of a chariot in a crash. They donned helmets of leather or felt and wound strips of leather or linen around their legs as protection against abrasions from the guard behind which they stood. Their chests were laced up with tight leather straps, as if they were wearing corsets.

A number of images show charioteers with knives thrust into the straps around their chest, which they could use to cut themselves loose if they were thrown out of a chariot and dragged along. This was far more likely to happen in Rome than in Greece, since Greek charioteers held the reins in both hands whereas the Romans tied the four pairs of relatively heavy reins around their torso, just above the waist. They steered their chariots by adjusting their weight and made further corrections with the left hand, holding the whip in the right.

Good charioteers must have been capable of true wizardry. They stood balanced precariously with only the semicircular guard in front to steady them, bracing their knees against it when necessary. The pull of taut reins exerted enormous pressure on the charioteer, and an unexpected move by one of the horses could cause a severe jolt to the chariot, and so it is perhaps unrealistic to compare Roman charioteers to today's featherweight jockeys. Presumably they were selected more for their muscle power, suppleness, and stamina. A few extra kilos would have been an advantage rather than a disadvantage to the driver of a *quadriga*.

CHAPTER 5

A Day at the Circus Maximus

On the day before the races there was a palpable sense of nervous tension at the racing stables. The charioteers went through one last training session with their horses, adjusting the draft pole, the position of the yoke, and the length of the reins as necessary, and otherwise took time out to rest. The chariots were subjected to a final check in the workshop, where the axles and wheels were carefully inspected once last time. Doctors and trainers examined the horses for any hidden injuries and sometimes made the difficult decision to replace a horse at the last moment. Nothing was left to chance.

After a night's sleep in their own stables around the Campus Martius, the horses were taken to special stables at the Circus Maximus shortly before the races in which they were to compete. Their own familiar stable lads stayed at their side throughout, doing all they could to put the animals at ease. They settled down to wait, until it was time to harness the teams and steer them toward the starting gates.

The crowd set out long before the first race. In the early hours a tremendous commotion developed around the Circus Maximus as 150,000 spectators shuffled toward the entrances. Roads became congested, unable to accommodate so many people. On all sides there was shouting and shrieking, which made the atmosphere quite frightening. Arriving at the circus, the vast crowd had to wait to be allowed in. Long lines developed, especially at the gates that led to the highest tiers of seating, where places were often available free of charge. Impatient, nervous spectators argued with each other. The poet Juvenal expressed horror at the fraught atmosphere around the Circus Maximus shortly before the races began. He believed a wealthy Roman could move safely through the crowd only if he was accompanied by several burly slaves as bodyguards.[1]

Sometimes an emperor in his palace on the Palatine, annoyed by the racket from the waiting throng, would try to calm people down. Caligula became truly furious one night at the noise echoing around his palace, keeping him awake, and sent soldiers to deal with the crowd. They laid into the massed spectators with clubs. Suetonius tells us they caused great slaughter, not just among the plebeians but among people who were clearly not there to get themselves free seats.[2] Twenty knights, as many women, and countless others were clubbed to death or crushed underfoot in the resulting panic. The eccentric emperor Heliogabalus reacted similarly two centuries later, although his approach was far more sophisticated than Caligula's. He released a large number of snakes among the waiting masses. The outcome was just as he had hoped. Terrible panic broke out as people fled in all directions. They tripped over each other, and many were trampled to death.[3]

Outside the Circus Maximus, and indeed inside, under the spans of the arches, spectators could buy all kinds of snacks, wine, bread, pastries, cold meats, vegetables, and fruit from innumerable stalls. There were souvenir shops selling images of the most popular charioteers in the colors of their factions and scale models of chariots. It is a scene we would immediately recognize from our own experiences at large football stadiums.

Juvenal and Cyprian paint a much more depressing and disconcerting picture of the environment in and around the Circus Maximus.[4] They make it sound as if pimps and prostitutes were the dominant figures at the circus, as if the Roman world's dark side was concentrated here on festival days. Cyprian, a Christian author who lived in the third century AD, goes even further. He has nothing good to say about these mass popular spectacles and claims that the entrance to the Circus Maximus ran straight through a large brothel. That was untrue, of course, as Cyprian knew perfectly well, but by making a connection between the Circus Maximus and prostitution he was hoping to deter Christians from visiting the racetrack.

Once inside the walls of the Circus Maximus, the spectators still had a long way to go before reaching their seats via flights of steps. Then they sat on the cushions they had brought with them to wait for the official opening, a solemn ceremony reminiscent of the triumphal processions of victorious generals, only in the opposite direction. A triumphator—a victorious general—would ride in a four-horse chariot from the Porta Triumphalis near the Campus Martius past the Circus Flaminius and the Velabrum along the Via Sacra to the Forum Romanum. He would pass the Circus Maximus and the Forum Boarium before riding on to the Capitol to offer thanks to Jupiter Capitolinus for his victory. In contrast, the organizer of a charioteering spectacle would begin his circus procession on the Capitol and ride across the Forum Romanum to the Circus Maximus.

It was always an impressive sight—the Romans spoke of the *pompa circensis*—when a long ceremonial procession made its way out of the catacombs into the full light of the arena to announce the entry of the organizer.[5] Out in front, boys from the highest social circles rode on horseback, followed on foot by boys who would later serve in the infantry. Then came the participants of the games, first the charioteers in their two- or four-horse chariots, next the jockeys and athletes of the secondary events on the program, wearing loin cloths, followed by a group clad in purple tunics, who bobbed into the arena dancing to the accompaniment of flutes and lyres. In their wake came a choir of satyrs, long-haired and clad in goatskins, and sileni in shaggy tunics.[6] After them came servants carrying censers, decorative amphorae, or statues of the temple gods, until finally the organizer entered the arena in full regalia, riding in a four-horse chariot, looking for all the world like that familiar figure the triumphator. After he had received the cheers of the crowds up in the packed stands, the opening ceremony ended with a sacrifice of bulls.

We can only wonder how the audience reacted to this spectacle. For many it would be the umpteenth occasion on which they had experienced the same ritual, and we might well imagine that after a few times they would be pretty tired of it. Yet it was part of a tradition they were obliged to respect. They could not permit themselves any blatant expressions of boredom, since the emperor would not tolerate disdainful remarks about the ceremony.

When the procession had withdrawn to the catacombs and the organizer was seated in the special place reserved for him, the races began. Each race was decided in seven laps of about 700 meters. The chariots circled the 340-meter-long *spina* seven times, and if we add another 160 meters from the starting gates to the *spina* and an extra 10 meters or so around each of the turning posts, the total length of a race comes to about 5,060 meters—for those in the lead, that is, and as long as they cut the bends tightly and skimmed the *spina* as closely as possible. The less successful charioteers were likely to be forced over toward the outside of the track and have to cover a significantly longer distance. Given that speeds of some seventy kilometers an hour were achieved on the straight and the drivers had to slow their horses for each turn, reducing speed to about thirty kilometers an hour, the winner must have crossed the finishing line after about nine or ten minutes.

There is no proper eyewitness account of a race at the Circus Maximus. Either literary authors did not think it worthwhile to give lengthy reports of this great passion of the common people, or they regarded it as beneath their dignity to admit to all and sundry that the races thrilled them. Those who did choose to write about the races had to take account of the fact that they would be looked at askance by some in their own circles if they expressed too much enthusiasm on the subject.

We therefore have to content ourselves with disparate comments, mere fragments of something approaching a report. The nearest thing we have to proper coverage is a story told by the poet Ovid. He admits he is no expert and says he actually found himself in the Circus Maximus by chance, accompanying a girl with whom he had fallen hopelessly in love. She watches the races intently, whereas he is interested mainly in her. After a few brief remarks about the solemn opening procession, he describes sharing the girl's feelings when her favorite charioteer appears on the track. He sees everything through her eyes:

> Now, they've cleared the course. The Praetor's starting the first race.
> Four-horse chariots. Look—they're off.
> There's your driver. Anyone *you* back is bound to win.
> Even the horses seem to know what you want.
> My God, he's taking the corner too wide.
> What are you doing? The man behind is drawing level.
> What are you doing, wretch? Breaking a poor girl's heart.
> For pity's sake pull on your left rein!

We've backed a loser. Come on everyone, all together,
flap your togas and signal a fresh start.
Look they're calling them back. Lean your head against me
so the waving togas don't disarrange your hair.
Now, they're off again—plunging out of the stalls,
rushing down the course in a clash of colors.
Now's your chance to take the lead. Go all out for that gap.
Give my girl and me what we want.
Hurrah, he's done it! You've got what you wanted, sweetheart.
That only leaves me—do I win too?
She's smiling. There's a promise in those bright eyes.
Let's leave now. You can pay my bet in private.[7]

Ovid gives us no more than a general impression, a good one certainly, but the events of the race largely pass him by. The only actual commentary that has come down to us does not refer to the Circus Maximus or any of the other great circuses of the Roman Empire but to a chariot race in the palace arena in Ravenna. It is a poem written in the fifth century by Sidonius Apollinaris, the bishop of Auvergne, and dedicated to a young friend, Consentius, who had won a race a short time before. Although this is a contest between "keen amateurs," Sidonius's story, rendered below in prose, contains sufficient factual detail to give us an impression of what must have happened on the great racetrack in the Circus Maximus when professional charioteers competed and how the audience must have reacted.

Phoebus began a new annual cycle and Janus with his two faces brought the *calendae* [the first of January] around once again, the day on which the new magistrates were to take their seats. On this particular day the emperor is in the habit of twice holding games, called private games. A host of young men, all from the court, offer a furious imitation of the field of Elis and their *quadrigae* swarm out across the track. The urn is already calling you and the eager cheers of the hoarse spectators get you going. Where the entrance gate stands and the magistrates' seats are to be found, with a wall all around and six covered stables on either side, within which are the starting stalls, you draw lots for one of the four chariots. You mount the chariot and take the loose reins in your hands. Your partner does likewise, as do the drivers on the opposing side. The colors by which the chariots can be identified, white and blue, green and red, stand out brightly.

The stable lads hold the horses' heads in their hands and grip the reins tightly and bind the curly manes into flexible plaits. As they do so they goad the steeds, pat them lovingly, stroke them, and work them up into a rapturous frenzy. The horses snort at the barrier and press against those sealed swinging doors, vapor steaming out through the planks in front of them, so that the track fills with their breath even before the race has begun. They push, they are nervous, they pull, they struggle, they are fiery, they jump, they are fearful and feared. They don't keep their feet still for a moment but kick their hooves against the hard wood.

At last the herald calls forth the impatient *quadrigae* with a loud trumpet blast, launching the fleet chariots into the field. The force of triple-forked lightning, the arrow shot from a Scythian bowstring, the trail of a shooting star, the leaden storm blast of pellets shot from catapults by the Balearians have never sped across the heavens so fast. The earth trembles under the wheels and the air is heavy with the dust flying up from the track. At the same time the charioteers crack their whips and hold tight to the reins.

And so they rush on, sticking their chests out in front of their chariots. They lash the yoke horses on the withers, not on the back. With the drivers leaning forward like that it's hard to see whether or not they are balancing more on the draft pole than on the chariot axles.

Now, having flown across the open part of the first lap, you disappear from sight as if on wings, to the other side of the artificially divided track, in the middle of which stretches the long, low double wall of the *euripus*. When all have passed the second turning post, which is farther out, your teammate catches up with the two others, who have already overtaken you. So according to the rules of the racetrack you are now in fourth place. The charioteers in the middle wait for the moment when the leading chariot drifts too far to the right, simply because it's going so fast, and they'll be able to pass it, or until the driver steers too far over toward the podium, leaving a gap on the inside.

You, however, lean forward, and with the utmost effort you keep good control of your four horses and wisely save their strength for the seventh lap. The others lash at their steeds and shout at them, and with every step the sweat pours from the drivers and their onward flying horses onto the ground. The raw shrieks of the enthralled crowd make hearts beat faster and all the contestants, both drivers and animals, grow hot with the thrill of the race and cold with fear. So they complete the first lap, then the second, the third, and the fourth.

But then, on the fifth lap, the man in the lead, no longer able to resist the pressure of his pursuers, steers his chariot aside, for he has seen in trying to egg on his fleet team that his yoke horses are exhausted. And the return half of the sixth lap is already almost over and the crowd is already clamoring for the awarding of prizes, and your opponents feel confident, expecting nothing more from you, and they speed on carefree along the track.

But suddenly you impose your will on the horses with slack reins; chest taut you step a little further forward and give your foaming steeds free rein, exactly as the famous charioteer [Pelops] did long ago when he dragged Oenomaus along with him and made all Pisa tremble. One of your opponents, trying to get around the turning post as tightly and by as short a route as he can, is pressed hard by you. Rattled as he is, he can no longer control his horses, which take the bend too fast. As he is thrown off course by their disarray, you pass him; you stay precisely on track.

The other driver, already acknowledging the cheers of the crowd, has drifted too far to the right toward the spectators in doing so. Too late he swerves his horses diagonally back toward the center, urging them on with his whip. He has been careless. Racing straight ahead you catch up with this rival too, even though he has left his direct course and is trying to stay in front of you, swerving at you. Recklessly he rushes at you and, believing that his teammate is still in first place, shamelessly drives sidelong at your chariot to push you aside. His horses fall forward, a tangle of legs ends up in the twelve spokes of his wheels, which are blocked with a loud cracking noise. The rims of the wheels shatter the trapped legs. He, the fifth victim, falls forward out of his crashing chariot, making the havoc he has created complete. Gushing blood disfigures his forehead.

Then a deafening noise arises, such as not even Mount Lycaeus can create with its cypress trees, nor the forests of Ossa with their many storms. Not even the seas of Sicily, rolling in with breakers driven by the south wind, make such a sound, any more than does the Propontis, whose wild waves enclose the Bosphorus. Now the righteous emperor calls for palm fronds, for silken robes of honor, necklaces, and wreaths to reward the performance. To the defeated, who are already discouraged enough, he awards carpets woven of multicolored hair.[8]

If even an amateur contest could be this exciting, what must it have been like in the Circus Maximus when one race after another reached its climax? At the beginning of the imperial era there were still only twelve races a day, and until the reign of Claudius (41–54) this was the standard number, although his predecessor, Caligula, had organized forty races on his birthday in the year 37.[9] In 46 Claudius increased the program of races to twenty-four,[10] and from then on this became the benchmark for organizers, although Nero did make one further attempt to hold more races in a day. Emperors Vespasian, Titus, and Domitian, too, felt that twenty-four races were not enough for a full day's entertainment and organized thirty races a day for a time. Even that was insufficient to satisfy Domitian. During the *ludi saeculares* in AD 88 ("secular games," sometimes called "centenary festivals," which were held at intervals of roughly 110 years), he put a hundred races on the daily program, although he reduced the distance to be covered from seven laps to five, thereby, or so he hoped, increasing the excitement.[11] These changes were not destined to last. After Domitian's death the program reverted to twenty-four races of seven laps of the track. In the fourth century this was still the usual number, as the Calendar of Philocalus of 354 indicates. In the sixth century Cassiodorus wrote that the Romans held twenty-four races to correspond with the twenty-four hours in a day.

Only very compelling circumstances, such as a radically worsening economy or a severe shortage of horses, could persuade the authorities to depart from the usual program. A substantial reduction in the number of races seems to have taken place under Emperor Septimius Severus for the *ludi saeculares* of 204. From surviving fragments of the festival records we can conclude that only seven races were held.[12] The reasons for this adjustment to the program are not given, but they would doubtless have been of a financial nature.

In circuses in provincial cities the number of races was probably reduced rather more often, sometimes for lack of the funding required for a full day's program but more often on orders from above. However eager an emperor was to hold chariot races, if the army ran short of good mounts, he had no choice but to send a document ordering horses to be made available to the soldiers. The racing stables at the Circus Maximus were usually spared, since every emperor knew that there would be a storm of protest if he ordered top racehorses to be taken from the stables on the Campus Martius. It would not do his reputation as "patron of all," as protector of the people of the city, any good. Dissatisfaction among provincial populations was less damaging to the emperor.

Although the spectators had come mainly to see races with four-horse chariots, there was always room on a day's program for races between *bigae* and *trigae*. An accompaniment to the main events, they were intended primarily to give young charioteers a chance to demonstrate what they could do in front of a large audience. Some organizers went to great lengths to serve up something new each time to the pampered spectators besides the usual *quadriga* racing, holding contests between six-, eight-, or even ten-horse chariots. It seems it was not unknown for chariots drawn by as many as twenty horses to appear on the racetrack. But whatever new variants were invented, the four-horse chariot races were always the main item.

At fixed intervals the races were interrupted by other entertainments. In early times the Trojan Game was popular, a kind of reenactment of the Trojan war. Two or three groups of armed riders would engage each other in combat. They fought mock battles on horseback, the aim being not to kill your opponent but to demonstrate riding skill and athleticism. The participants were boys from prominent families, and this was a chance for them to show what they were made of. The game was not without its risks. Suetonius describes how Nonius Asprenas was lamed by a fall from his horse and received a gold collar (*torques*) from Emperor Augustus in compensation, along with permission for him and his descendants to add the honorable title *Torquatus* to their name.[13] Whether this event was featured in shows put on by emperors who came after Augustus we cannot be certain. When Asinius Pollio complained bitterly to Augustus that his grandson Aeserninus had broken a leg, the emperor took the game off the program. There is no further mention of the Trojan Game after that, and so it seems likely it was discontinued.

The *desultores* (acrobats on horseback) enjoyed great popularity, too. Both as jockeys and as performers of feats that were both artistic and courageous, they reaped huge applause. They did circus acts, jumping from one galloping horse to another, hanging under the belly of a horse, or standing on a horse's back and making it dance. But true horse lovers preferred to see riders in actual races, and the organizers adjusted the program accordingly. In most circus shows one horseracing event was held for every five chariot races. The distance covered is not known, but it would certainly have been less than the seven laps of the chariot races. The prize money reflected this. During the *ludi saeculares* held by Septimius Severus in 204 the winning rider was awarded 6,000 sestertii, the rider in second place 2,000, and the man who came third 1,000—not a great deal compared with the main prize of 24,000 sestertii that went to the winner of a *quadriga* race.

A race known as the *diversium* must have been an extraordinary event. Sadly, the authors of the time tell us little about it, perhaps because it was not part of the program at the Circus Maximus as often as it was later featured at the Hippodrome in Constantinople, but it was undoubtedly spectacular. It took the form of a duel between champions, between the numbers one and two in a race that had just finished. The participants knew they were putting their reputation on the line by signing up for it. The event involved two races. In the first the drivers used their own four-horse chariots; for the second they switched chariots and horses. Clumsy accidents were a feature of the second race, since horses did not readily allow themselves to be steered by an unfamiliar hand. Another thrilling event was the *pedibus ad quadrigam*, a normal race except for the finish. The charioteers first covered several laps in their racing chariots, then after crossing the finishing line they jumped out to cover one or more laps of the track at a sprint to determine the winner.[14]

These mixed events may have looked spectacular, but the crowds were there to see the four-horse chariot races. Long before the *quadrigae* set off down the track, the staff of the racing stables would engage in a "cold war," using all acceptable and some unacceptable means. Sabotage and threats by drivers, trainers, or stable hands: anything that might help to defeat your opponent was part of the game. But from the moment the starting signal was given for a race, the outcome was down to the charioteers and their horses.

The very first race, immediately after the opening ceremony, was one of the main events, with top drivers from all four stables. Putting them first on the program offered a major advantage in that famous horses and drivers could perform again later in the day, occasionally against the same opponents, usually against others.

The organizers were well aware that they needed to do all they could to guarantee that the races were conducted fairly. A proper starting procedure was the first requirement. To prevent chariots from the same stable taking up favorable starting positions next to each other, places at the starting line were decided by drawing lots. An umpire put four small balls in the colors of the stables into an urn, then stuck a stick through the handles and upended the urn so that the balls rolled out. The driver whose color emerged first chose a starting stall, then the second, and so on. This procedure was repeated until the starting positions of all eight or twelve chariots had been decided.

Stable lads accompanied the chariots and their drivers to the allotted starting stalls. Then attention turned to the presiding magistrate. Sitting on a platform directly above the starting gates, he signaled the beginning of the race by dropping the *mappa*, a white flag. This white cloth is in some ways reminiscent of the black-and-white checkered flag used in formula one motor racing, except that the drivers in the stalls could not see it and had to rely on watching the response of the *moratores*, their helpers, and waiting for a signal from them. Whether this starting procedure was used from the earliest times or introduced later we have no way of knowing. The only author to say anything about it is the sixth-century Cassiodorus, who attributes the founding of the custom to Nero. He writes that one day the spectators were in their seats waiting for the races to start, but Nero in his loge had not yet finished his sumptuous breakfast. When the spectators grew restless and increasingly rowdy, Nero is said to have thrown his napkin down into the arena to indicate that the racing could begin.[15]

At the fall of the flag the *moratores* immediately threw open the locks holding the swinging doors shut. The chariots poured out and a deafening racket erupted up in the stands. This procedure usually went off without any problems, but false starts, such as the one in the race described by Ovid, undoubtedly occurred. If the race was blatantly unfair as a result, the crowd would express its dissatisfaction by jeering, and the head umpire would be compelled to call the chariots back to their starting positions, which must have been quite a job in the hellish tumult.

Sometimes accidents occurred even in the starting stalls. One such unlucky charioteer was called Corax. During the *ludi saeculares* held by Emperor Claudius he was flung out of his chariot while waiting in his stall for the signal for the gates to be opened. Had the horses been overcome by nerves, or was agitation on the part of the driver to blame? Pliny the Elder, whose anecdote this is, does not tell us.[16] He does say that the well-prepared but driverless horses shot out of the stall and took the lead in the field. They obstructed the other horses and raced in exactly the way they would have done had Corax been standing in the chariot, stopping only after passing the finishing line, having completed seven laps of the track. They were not declared to have won, however, since the rules stated that their driver had to cross the finishing line with them.

In the first 160 meters the charioteers needed great self-control. There was always a risk of mishap. The umpires watched closely to check that the horses were keeping to their marked lanes; only when they reached the first of the two *metae* were the drivers allowed to take the ideal course and pass as close as they could to the *spina*. If they left their lanes any earlier, they would automatically be disqualified. After that, virtually anything went. They could cut in front of each other, fan out across the full breadth of the track, or deliberately crash into other chariots. The drivers might even use violence, not against each other—

that was punishable with immediate disqualification—but against their opponents' horses, which they lashed with their whips. This made the horses skittish. Turning their head away, they were diverted from their course. Sometimes the lashes were so fierce that a horse suffered an eye injury. A vet called Pelagonius relates that of the thirty-five salves and ointments he used to treat eye problems in horses, fourteen were specifically intended to heal eye injuries incurred on the racetrack.

It quickly became clear which of the competitors had no chance of winning. At the far end of the *spina* on the first lap the chariots would still be close together as they approached the three pillars at the turning point. Since they all wanted to turn as tightly as possible and the distances between them were still small, there was tremendous congestion. They usually emerged in one piece, since well-trained charioteers were accustomed to driving in close proximity, but sometimes one or more met with disaster, either by accident or by design. Combined efforts were important here. Drivers from the same stable would agree beforehand that during a race with twelve chariots, three from each stable, two would concentrate on obstructing opponents, thereby increasing their leading man's chances of victory.

Sometimes the results of a collision were limited to material damage, and the tangled chariots, no longer able to move in any direction, were dragged out of the way as quickly as possible while the race continued. Often, however, a driver must have met a cruel fate when the horses caught up in the wreckage of a crashed chariot did not stop but powered on ahead. The reins were wound around the driver's waist, which meant that the first thing he had to do was to cut himself loose with the knife lodged in the leather straps across his chest. He often failed. Many were thrown out of their chariot and dragged along the ground behind or beside it. The most favorable outcome for the unfortunate driver was to survive the accident and emerge relatively unscathed. He was quite likely to pay with his life.

We know a few of the casualties of these crashes by name, such as the famous charioteer Flavius Scorpus. His life ended when his chariot was smashed to pieces just short of the finishing line. He was only twenty-seven years old, but he had notched up 2,048 victories in the course of his career.[17] Martial wrote his epitaph:

Here I lie, Scorpus, glory of the noisy Circus,
Darling of Rome. Yet how short-lived my fame!
At twenty-seven I died—still young, truth be told,
Yet Fate counted my victories and thought me very old.[18]

The inscription on the grave of another charioteer, the very young Florus, suggests he had little chance to derive any pleasure from his performances on the racetrack. Before his career had properly started, it was over: "Here I, Florus, a still youthful charioteer, lie buried. As I accelerated I fell out of my chariot into the shade of the underworld."[19] He was so young that the inscription records him as being a *bigarius infans*, still a child, allowed to race only in a two-horse chariot.

Sometimes a driver survived a bad accident with injuries so severe that he was left with lasting disabilities that forced him to retire. Broken bones in particular, which were difficult to treat, led to physical infirmities that would make a man unfit to drive a racing chariot. Less visible problems, too, such as torn ankle ligaments and hamstrings, wrenched muscles, or back injuries, could put a premature end to a driver's career. The degree to which the ancients struggled to treat these ailments is clear from the remedy Pliny the Elder advocated for the cure of minor injuries.[20] He advised that in the case of torn muscles and grazed skin the sore spot should be smeared with the dung of a wild boar, either dried or boiled in vinegar. Some doctors even went so far as to crush the droppings or incinerate them and then prescribe them to patients to be taken in a cup of water.

The horses often met with a far worse fate. They impacted hard on the wheels of other chariots or stepped on the wreckage left by a crash, spraining, wrenching, or breaking their legs. The two outer horses were exposed to the greatest danger, since they could be crushed under the wheels of other chariots. The horse to the left, called upon to take the turns most sharply, ran the additional risk of being squeezed against the *spina* or the *metae*. Complete recovery could not be expected in such cases, and a horse had to be in optimal condition to have any chance of victory in the circus. Those whose injuries were not particularly serious were transferred to one of the many stud farms. The rest were put down.

The jostling at the turns was fully visible only to certain sections of the crowd. Those spectators who were sitting at the end of the circus or on the long sides not too far from the *metae* could see the order in which the chariots were racing toward the turn. The rest could tell from the swelling noise whether the chariot in the lead belonged to the Greens, the Blues, the Reds, or the Whites. The names of the charioteers and their horses resounded across the arena. The spectators on the other side of the arena would take up the cry and chant in their turn the names of their favorites as soon as they came into sight. But a race lasted a long time, and no one could have any real confidence that the chariot in the lead after the first lap would be first across the finishing line. A charioteer might have overestimated the strength of his horses and exhausted them, or he might yet be put out of the running by the failure of his vehicle, or, most commonly of all, a driver in pursuit might have judged the capacities of his horses rather better and catch up after trailing initially.

Experienced spectators could sometimes see well in advance how a race was going to develop. The way a charioteer was driving told them enough. The poet Silius Italicus of the first century AD describes how during games held to commemorate the victory of the great Scipio Africanus over the Carthaginians some spectators quite quickly realized that Cyrnus, who had taken the lead in a *quadriga* race, was not going to win. While most of the crowd still thought he would maintain his lead, the aficionados made clear by their comments that things were not going well for him. They shouted that he was wasting his forces, that he was covering far too much distance in his efforts to cut across his opponents. But however loudly they yelled at him to spare his horses and fall back, he ignored them. Instead of reining in, he tried to maintain his lead. Their concerns proved well founded. Cyrnus had asked too much of his horses, and eventually the other chariots passed him.[21]

The lowering of the stone eggs or dolphins on the *spina* told the spectators how many laps had already been completed, and so they knew when a race was approaching its climax. If the final laps were truly thrilling, all the supporters' groups shouted at once. The staff of the stables sat together nervously, close to the track, waiting for the denouement. The *hortatores* were given their final instructions and rode on horseback between the chariots to pass on their orders. In the final two laps the drivers drew every last drop of strength from their

Formal ceremony. Accompanied by a tuba player, the organizer of the games approaches the winning charioteer, still in his *quadriga*, to present him with an olive branch and a laurel wreath. (Photograph by Jerzy Strzelecki)

horses. They gave free rein, stepped up the pace, and took great risks at the turns. All that counted for the driver in the lead now was victory. He would stop at nothing in his efforts to eliminate his challengers. Sometimes he succeeded, sometimes the leader was hoist with his own petard and crashed within sight of the finish. The Romans used the term *naufragium* to describe such an outcome: his chariot lay in pieces in the arena like a shipwreck.

Scribes employed by the organizers kept a precise record of how each victory was won. If their entries included the phrase *occupavit et vicit*, everyone knew that the winning charioteer had been in the lead from start to finish. If the man out in front was passed by a driver who had been at the back of the pack for several laps, beside his name was written *successit et vicit*. The most exciting kind of finish was always one in which the leading chariot was overtaken on the homestretch. The term for this was *erupit et vicit*, which made clear to everybody that the winner had been in second place for a long time before passing the leader just short of the finishing line.

Every race ended with a formal ceremony, and in contrast to our contemporary custom it was focused exclusively on the winner. His supporters were ecstatic. A second or third place was regarded as a defeat by both the driver and his supporters. As the losers quietly left the arena, the victorious charioteer rode a lap of honor, sometimes with his entire *quadriga*, sometimes seated on one of the winning horses, usually one of the trace horses. In front of the emperor's loge he gave a salute before walking up the steps to receive his prize directly from the emperor or the organizer of the games: an olive branch and a laurel wreath, along with a financial reward of between 30,000 and 60,000 sestertii, an enormous sum. Disappointment at their defeat was quickly over for those in second or third place, since they too were given sums of money greater than most people in Rome could earn in a lifetime.

There were reasonably lengthy intervals between races. The entrance and presentation of the four-horse chariots before each race took quite a while, as did the tributes paid to the prizewinners afterward, but most of the time was taken up with preparing the arena for the next race. Twelve *quadrigae* battling it out churned up the ground considerably, and since the crowd wanted to see fast races, the track had to be made level again. If fragments of crashed chariots had to be cleared away, it would take even longer for the course to be made ready.

The races went on until nightfall. After the official end of a day's racing the circus slowly emptied, and the spectators set off for home or went in search of a good time in one of the many bars, where supporters of the racing stable with most victories in the main events would make an appropriate amount of noise. Everywhere people talked until deep into the night about the races, the horses, and above all the charioteers. Reputations had been established or broken, new stars had come to the fore. Supporters of the losers were jeered, laughed at, and taunted. Sometimes they shrugged it off, sometimes they slunk away, but time and again they were unable to control themselves and went looking for a fight. The Praetorian Guard and the city cohorts would have to intervene to restore order. So a day at the Circus Maximus often ended in chaos. Fortunately the fans never had to wait very long for the next opportunity to display their devotion to their favorite charioteers. Within one or two weeks there would be a fresh series of races and a fresh chance to triumph.

CHAPTER 6

The Heroes
of the Arena

Social Status

Absolutely top-ranking charioteers could acquire a star status comparable to that of today's famous football players, tennis players, cyclists,
and jockeys. They were admired and revered and sometimes became
fabulously rich. With such prestige on offer it seems curious that the
pool of talent the stables were able to draw upon was small. Attempts
have been made in the past to show that charioteers came from all
strata of the population, but the latest research makes it clear that this
was not the case. Based on 229 surviving epitaphs and honor inscriptions for more or less successful charioteers, Gerhard Horsmann has
shown that recruitment was limited to the bottom ranks of Roman society: slaves and freedmen.[1] More than half of all the inscriptions state
explicitly that the driver was a *servus* (slave) or *libertus* (freedman).
Very often there is no way of discovering the status of the charioteer
referred to, and of only twenty-one can we say with certainty that they
were in possession of citizenship and bore the three Roman names that
distinguished a Roman citizen. Of those twenty-one, twelve initially
had the status of freedmen and only later became citizens.

The vast majority of charioteers, in contrast to those few who were
Roman citizens, had only one name, usually a typical slave name, de-
rived from a mythological or historical figure: Alexander, Castor, Cre-
scens, Diocles, Dionysius, Epaphroditus, Euhemerus, Eutyches, Felix,
Fortunatus, Fuscus, Hierax, Menander, Narcissus, Olympus, Orpheus,
Philippus, Polyphemus, Protus, Pyramus, Salutaris, Scirtus, Scorpus,
Venustus, or Zeno. Of course we cannot exclude the possibility that

a charioteer with a higher status might have used a stage name in the arena, but there is no indication that this happened on a significant scale.

Many charioteers were the sons of slaves (illegitimate by definition) and had first been attached to one of the factions as drivers, stable lads, grooms, masseurs, or simply cleaners. From early youth they had learned how to handle horses. Once old enough to take the reins, they would climb into a chariot and ride around the training complex. Slaves with other backgrounds were sought out, too, or brought to the stables by slave owners motivated by pure greed (after all, there was money to be made). Most prospective charioteers responded with enthusiasm, since a performance as the driver of a four-horse chariot was the dream of every slave. It offered him the opportunity eventually to buy his freedom, marry, start a family, and command some degree of respect.

This raises the question as to why freeborn men were in such a small minority, no more than a couple of percent of the total. The answer lies in the public image of the charioteering profession, which, despite the popularity of its top drivers, was low. For most Romans the sport was closely associated with slave status. Except for a few megastars, charioteers were *infamis*, disreputable, like actors and gladiators. Roman citizens knew that by applying to join one of the racing stables they were jeopardizing their status. Despite sometimes extreme poverty, this was a step further than most were prepared to go. If they did decide to abandon their miserable circumstances for a life on the racetrack—and it is conceivable that the thought might quite commonly have occurred to them—the authorities made every effort to dissuade them from such a course. From the third century BC, when monetary prizes became more important than the honor attached to a victory, charioteers, like actors, were regarded as practitioners of an *ars ludicra*, a reprehensible art, from which anyone with a modicum of social standing was expected to keep his distance. To make sure that citizens stuck to the right path, all kinds of legal stipulations were introduced that not only labeled charioteers inferior but blocked them from any advancement in the fields of law and politics.

It is difficult to tell whether these measures worked. At first sight it seems they did, since, although top drivers were popular heroes in the early imperial period, few people succumbed to the temptation of a life

on the racetrack. But when we read that in 19 and 11 BC special reso-
lutions in the Senate were needed to keep freeborn men from signing
up for the races, it becomes clear that dissuasion had failed and firm
measures were required. From then on freeborn men were forbidden
to practice any of the reprehensible arts before the age of twenty-five.[2]
This meant it was practically impossible for them to become successful
charioteers, since at that age it was far too late to make the switch and
compete with drivers who had been active on the track from their earliest youth. It was as good as impossible to catch up on ten years of lost
ground, while only the prospect of gaining the kind of status enjoyed by
the greatest of charioteers could motivate a man to relinquish his civic
freedoms.

Senators (and emperors) had even more reason to be dissuaded than
ordinary Romans. It was absolutely incompatible with their social status to compete in races against slaves and freedmen. Nevertheless, they
could not resist the call of the racetrack completely, and both senators
and emperors are known to have driven racing chariots, not in official
races but in other Roman circuses, screened off from the public.

Career

Virtually every charioteer with a reasonable number of victories to his
name would insist on being given an epitaph or an inscription of honor.
Considering the competitive nature of Roman society, it is easy to understand the importance a driver attributed to this kind of memorial.
After his death his family and friends would immortalize his exploits
in short texts carved in stone, which for all their brevity can sometimes
offer an illuminating insight into the sporting life led by the deceased
charioteer. If his offspring had not themselves been able to keep a careful record of his accomplishments, they could always base his epitaph
on the records maintained by the staff of the Circus Maximus, which
not only gave the results of each race but noted precisely what kind of
contest it was: whether *quadrigae*, *trigae*, or *bigae* were involved, how
many teams from each stable took part, what the victorious horses
were called, and whether the winner had been first from the start or had
taken the lead on the homestretch.

Good charioteers made their mark while they were young. The epitaph carved for the slave Crescens, a great talent who died at the age of twenty-two,[3] tells us that he started racing when he was thirteen, probably in the junior contests with two-horse chariots. He then drove three-horse chariots, with two horses under the yoke and one on the trace, as preparation for the great challenge of the *quadriga* race, with two trace horses. He achieved his first victory in a four-horse chariot in 115, when he was not yet fourteen. In total, in the more than nine years he was active (from 115 to 124), he drove in 686 races. On 47 occasions he crossed the finishing line in the lead, 130 times he was second, and 111 times he came in third. His prize money amounted to 1,558,346 sestertii, an enormous sum considering his career ended so abruptly, probably with an accident. It is striking that despite his youth he achieved nineteen of his victories in races in which only one chariot was fielded per racing stable. This attests to his great talent, since young charioteers were usually entered for races involving several chariots per racing stable, driving not to win but to follow orders for the benefit of their stable's leading man. This changed once they had a number of honorable placements to their name. From then on they could concentrate on their own success.

At the Circus Maximus the less talented, more mediocre drivers were usually deployed in sideshows, while others appeared in provincial circuses where the monetary prizes were significantly smaller and the organizers therefore had more difficulty attracting top charioteers. They lived in fear of being taken out of the chariots because they had been unsuccessful for too long and downgraded to stable lad or groom. Such lesser talents did not have great careers to look forward to, and on their death no eye-catching monuments would be built for them, with elaborate inscriptions describing their achievements. If they were given gravestones at all, the expense would be met by the *familia quadrigaria*, a group of drivers of four-horse teams within a racing stable, which would add to the inscription a statement saying its members had paid for the gravestone out of their own pocket to honor a dearly departed colleague.

The winners led very different lives. Inglorious persons of low social repute at the start of their careers, they were utterly transformed after just a few victories and began behaving like sporting heroes. They took it for granted that a great deal of prize money was in prospect, but first they had to overcome a number of obstacles. While they were slaves, they could not actually get their hands on their prize money, as it was paid out to their owners. It was therefore crucial to gain freedom from slavery as quickly as possible. Being freed took time, however. For some the whole process was completed rather sooner than for others.

Between the slave owner and the charioteer an agreement would be made that emancipation was to take place after a specific sum had been paid. A couple of major prizes must have been sufficient. Under normal circumstances slaves in Roman society were freed only after they passed the age of thirty, but in the case of a top charioteer this rule would be set aside, partly because of the great risks he ran on the racetrack but no doubt also because with prizes of between 15,000 and 60,000 sestertii he was able to earn the sum required for his emancipation very quickly. If the owner refused to free him within a reasonable period, this would be pointed out to the owner in no uncertain terms by supporters during the races. He would bow to pressure and agree to free the slave.

From the surviving epitaphs we cannot tell what percentage of charioteers managed to raise their status from slave to freedman. Some inscriptions say nothing about the transition at all; others mention it explicitly. The gravestone carved according to his own instructions for Epaphroditus, a charioteer at the time of Emperor Domitian, records that he achieved 178 victories for the Reds while he was still a slave and then, *as a free man*, won another eight times for the Purples—a faction that existed only under Domitian—before meeting his dark fate in death.[4]

Once emancipated, a charioteer was free to negotiate with the leaders of his racing stable as to how the prize money would be divided up. Only a top charioteer who could brandish offers from one of the other racing stables could make steep demands; if he was no better than average, he had to proceed with caution. After all, he was driving horses that belonged to and had been carefully nurtured by his racing stable, he made use of the training complex, and he enjoyed free medical support from doctors and masseurs. Although the inscriptions say nothing about how the winnings were shared and literary authors are silent on the subject, I think a charioteer would have worked out a distributive formula with the head of a racing stable. His boss had every interest in

Head of a charioteer. (Photograph by Jastrow)

keeping a good driver in his stable, and so he would usually offer realistic conditions, in the knowledge that if he overplayed his hand there was a fair chance the relationship would be damaged and the charioteer would seek contact with other stables.

No matter how well a racing stable treated its drivers, they sometimes proved impossible to keep and were bought up by rival stables. Inscriptions have been found in which reasonably successful charioteers or their descendants describe the high points of their careers, and these show that many seized the opportunity to switch to a different stable, improving their financial position by doing so. Take the career of two brothers who died young. They were good drivers, the older of the two especially, and sons of a famous charioteer, Polyneices. After their early deaths their grieving father had statues erected to commemorate his sons. The statues have since been lost, but the text in which their triumphs are recorded has survived:

> Marcus Aurelius Polyneices, born a slave, lived for 29 years,
> 9 months, and 2 days. He achieved 739 victories: for the Reds
> 655, for the Greens 55, for the Blues 12, for the Whites 17. Three
> of his victories were achieved with six-horse teams, eight with
> eight-horse teams, and nine with ten-horse teams.

> Marcus Aurelius Mollicius Tatianus, born a slave, lived for 20
> years, 8 months, and 7 days. He achieved 125 victories: 89 for the
> Reds, 24 for the Greens, 5 for the Blues, and 7 for the Whites.[5]

It is striking that the younger brother, at only twenty, had driven for all four of the racing stables. This can be explained only by assuming that he followed his famous older brother, whose career probably went as follows. He drove for the relatively minor stable of the Whites until he was bought by the Blues. His reputation apparently grew, and after a while he was signed up by the Greens, before going on to race until his death, for a great deal of money, for the Reds, for whom he achieved 655 victories.

None of this was in store for a driver with only a few victories to his name. Scirtus, for instance. In the thirteen years he was active as a charioteer, between AD 13 and 25, he managed only seven victories for the Whites.[6] It is understandable, given this meager result, that he was never granted the opportunity to drive for a different stable.

Charioteers ran such risks that it was inevitable many of their careers would end early, before they turned thirty, often with death in a crash. Sometimes a brilliant career was cut short by a fatal illness. Such was the fate of Eutyches of Tarraco, a young driver who was expected to reach the top. His epitaph tells of his promising early career: "In this grave rest the remains of a beginner on the racetrack, who nevertheless was far from incompetent in handling the reins. I already had the courage to try my hand at driving *quadrigae*, although I was still racing in *bigae*."[7] There were, of course, charioteers who ended their career wealthy and in good health, surrounded by great luxury. We are talking here about the absolute top rank, men with many hundreds of wins to their name—sometimes more than a thousand. A thousand victories was seen as a milestone. The lucky few could glory in the title *milliarius* (thousander), making clear to all that they had accomplished an extraordinary feat. Some went well beyond the thousand mark. Out ahead of the pack are Flavius Scorpus and Pompeius Musclosus with 2,048 and 3,599 victories, respectively. Yet they have not gone down in history as the most successful charioteers of all time. That honor is reserved for Publius Aelius Calpurnianus Gutta and Gaius Appuleius Diocles, both of whom lived in the first half of the second century. We know about their achievements from two lengthy inscriptions that record all their victories. Scorpus and Musclosus were granted only comparatively brief inscriptions, in which the number of their victories is given but without any elucidation.

Calpurnianus is in fact a special case, since he was one of the very few charioteers of free birth. Either he was a child of parents both of whom had Roman citizenship, or he was a foreigner (*peregrinus*) who had been made a Roman citizen by Hadrian on account of his great exploits. His inscription of honor belongs to a grave monument that once stood on the Via Flaminia. The monument, which Calpurnianus probably erected himself when he left the racetrack, has been lost, but a large portion of the text of the inscription was preserved in a medieval manuscript. We read that Calpurnianus celebrated 1,127 victories. For 1,117 of them we are able to say for which stable and in what type of race they were won:[8]

	White	Red	Blue	Green
1 chariot per stable	83	42	334	116
2 chariots per stable	7	32	184	184
3 chariots per stable	2	3	65	64
4 chariots per stable	0	1	0	0
	92	78	583	364

Immediately noticeable is the fact that Calpurnianus achieved the greatest number of victories in races with just one chariot per stable, in which he could not rely on help from colleagues, and that in races with four chariots per stable he was victorious only once. Calpurnianus also recorded that he rode almost exclusively in four-horse chariots, only eight times in a three-horse chariot.

Calpurnianus did not forget to credit his horses; the most successful of them are named. Of his 583 victories for the Blues, just four animals acting as "main horse" were responsible for 309: Geminator was a member of the winning four-horse team on 92 occasions, Silvanus 103 times, Nitidus 52 times, and Saxo 60 times. The main horses that helped him to win for the Greens are named in the inscription, too: Danaus won 19 races, Oceanus 209, Victor 129, and Vindex 157. The total for these four horses comes to 814, many more than the 364 victories that Calpurnianus achieved in total for the Greens. A mistake may have crept into one of the figures, but it is equally likely that the horses were victorious not only with Calpurnianus but with other charioteers for the Greens.

We are in an even better position to follow the career of Diocles, from Lusitania in Spain, as a result of the long, if occasionally rather fragmentary, text on a monument erected in his honor when he took his leave of the racetrack. He was then forty-two and had entertained the public for twenty-four years. In that time he had built up a phenomenal list of achievements. The text tells us that he began his career in 122, at the age of eighteen, in a race for the White stable, winning for the first time two years later. In 128 he went over to the Greens and in 131 to the Reds, for whom he raced for the rest of his long career, which lasted until 146. Because the text breaks off in places, we cannot tell in which years he achieved his many victories for the Blues.

In total he lined up at the starting gates 4,257 times, making an average of 177 appearances a year. He passed the finishing line in the lead in 1,462 races, came in second in 861, and was third in 576. In 1,951 races he was not among the prizewinners. The part of the text giving the total number of victories he achieved for the different racing stables is incomplete, in that we can see he won 216 times for the Greens, 205 times for the Blues, and 81 times for the Whites, but no mention is made of the Reds. Since he won 1,462 races altogether, he must have achieved 960 victories for the Reds. That he was one of the true greats is also clear from the fact that he won 1,064 *quadriga* races in which only one chariot per stable took part. His victories in two- and three-horse chariots, six and four of them, respectively, form only a tiny fraction of the total. There was one day on which he raced twice in a six-horse chariot and once in a seven-horse chariot, winning all three times.

The text also has a certain amount to say about the manner in which Diocles' victories came about. He drove 815 times in the lead from start to finish, on 67 occasions he emerged from the back of the pack to pull ahead and win, in 502 races he was in second place for a long time before passing the leader on the final straight, and 36 times he watched from behind as others fought it out and then moved ahead just before the finish. One victory is of particular note. He was driving in a race that involved several chariots per stable. According to agreements within his stable, he was *praemissus*, which literally translates as "sent ahead," indicating that he acted as the pacesetter, or hare. This means that as part of a tactic familiar to us from the marathon or the ten thousand meters in modern athletics, he was expected to set the pace for a while before falling back or dropping out, at which point a colleague from his stable would finish the job. But he stayed in the lead and won.

Diocles, too, immortalized his successful horses. Nine of them pulled a winning chariot 100 times or more; one horse was part of a winning *quadriga* team on 200 occasions. Top horses Abigeius, Lucidus, Pompeianus, Cotynus, and Galata raced as yoke horses in 445 of Diocles' victories.

Prize Money

Diocles frankly admits there were charioteers before him who had achieved a larger number of victories. He is referring to Flavius Scorpus, who died tragically on the racetrack as we have seen, and to Pompeius Musclosus. It may seem odd that Diocles referred to them at all, since mentioning their names would surely do nothing to enhance his own star status, but evidently Diocles was interested not in honor alone but in boasting about his material rewards as well. He proudly tells us that his prize money was greater than that of any of his predecessors. This, too, is typical of Roman society, in which a high earner made no secret of his financial success.

The inscriptions on monuments erected in honor of Calpurnianus and Diocles make repeated mention of the *praemia maiora*, the first prizes. A victory rendered a sum of between 15,000 and 60,000 sestertii, second place half that amount. All in all Calpurnianus earned 1,230,000 sestertii in first prizes in his long career. His total earnings were far higher, however, since the smaller sums for second and third places are not included in these listings.

However much Calpurnianus's prize money came to, it was far less than the total sum won by Diocles, who earned a fortune in first prizes alone. He and his fans proudly recorded that he had won ninety-two *quadriga* races that carried prize money of between 30,000 and 60,000 sestertii:

> 32 times 30,000 sestertii = 960,000 sestertii
> 28 times 40,000 sestertii = 1,120,000 sestertii
> 29 times 50,000 sestertii = 1,450,000 sestertii
> 3 times 60,000 sestertii = 180,000 sestertii

This means that Diocles won a total of 3,710,000 sestertii in first prizes. Add to that the 60,000 sestertii he garnered for his victories in three-horse chariots, and his winnings come to 3,770,000 sestertii, three times the prize money Calpurnianus received for all his many first prizes, but even so only a fraction of Diocles' own total winnings during those years. The inscription explicitly states that he amassed the astronomical fortune of 35,863,120 sestertii. If we divide that sum by 4,257, the number of times he lined up at the starting gates, we see that on average he won 8,425 sestertii per race.

Just how wealthy Calpurnianus and Diocles were by the end of their career becomes clear when we compare their prize money with the incomes of Romans from different strata of the population. Naturally we have to be somewhat cautious here, since imperial Rome was subject to protracted inflation and sums of money cannot be compared across the centuries in a straightforward manner, but broadly speaking the figures are a useful guide.

The minimum annual income a person needed for basic subsistence at the start of the imperial era was 100 to 125 sestertii. A simple soldier earned between 900 and 1,200 sestertii a year, and successful artisans brought in between 700 and 2,300 sestertii. So in an average race Diocles earned the equivalent of eight times the annual income of a soldier or craftsman. A first prize of 50,000 sestertii left him holding a sum that a wage earner could come nowhere close to scraping together in his entire life.

Even wealthy Romans and members of the elite will have looked with envy at the earnings of top charioteers. Calpurnianus and Diocles sometimes pocketed with just one victory the equivalent of the annual income of a senior army officer. The income of the procurators (Roman government officials of the knightly class), at 100,000 to 300,000 sestertii a year, was to them a question of a few weeks or months of racing. There were senators with large estates who must have been envious of the wealthiest charioteers. A "lowly" senator had an annual income of between 70,000 and 480,000 sestertii from his property, an average senator 1 million. Only one senator, the fabulously rich Seneca with his annual income of 18 million sestertii, received revenue that far outstripped Diocles' earnings.[9]

The response within intellectual circles to the high monetary prizes available to charioteers is reflected in the slightly vindictive comments of poets Martial and Juvenal. Juvenal remarks that a hundred lawyers cannot match the wealth of the charioteer Lacerta, a star of the Reds.[10] Martial compares his own income with that of top charioteers. He writes with barely concealed envy that their winnings are utterly disproportionate. Whereas he receives a daily grant from his patron of 100 quadrantes (6.25 sestertii), so that he is free of day-to-day worries and can concentrate on writing poems, the charioteer Scorpus is awarded fifteen bags of gold for a single victory. Martial is probably referring to a first prize of 15,000 sestertii. The charioteer can parade about in splendid purple robes, while the poet has to make do with shabby clothing.[11] The unfairness seems really to have stuck in Martial's craw, since he also tells of a praetor who was unable to fulfill the request of a friend to lend him the 100,000 sestertii he needed in order to pay the census that would qualify him as a member of the knightly class. The reason: he needed the money to cover the cost of prizes for the charioteers Scorpus and Thallus.[12]

Martial may have been critical of the exorbitant earnings of these particular drivers, but that did not prevent him from elaborately praising Scorpus after the fatal accident on the racetrack, declaring his enormous appreciation for the charioteer's performances. He did so in two epigrams. The first is in chapter 5 of this book. In the second he is unrestrained in his expressions of sorrow at the loss of this great charioteer:

> Break, Victory, the palms of your renown;
> Let Favor beat herself upon her naked breast
> Honor itself wears mourning now. Let Glory weep
> And cast the crown that decked her locks into the flames.
> Robbed of your youthful prime, oh, such a shame!
> Scorpus, yoke up the black steeds now and drive . . .
> You drove so swiftly once, right to the finishing line,
> Why did you have to finish your life's race so soon?[13]

Martial's writings reflect the ambivalent attitude to chariot racing that prevailed in Roman society. On the one hand there was admiration for the sporting performances of the charioteers, on the other a widespread feeling that their earnings were astonishingly high, indeed excessively so. But this does not mean there was pressure to put an end to the practice. Even in times of financial crisis those responsible were more likely to consider reducing the number of races than lowering the prize money significantly. The organizers probably had no choice, since top charioteers were popular heroes and as such more or less sacrosanct. They would no doubt have responded to a cap on their earnings by going on strike.

The supporters would have rebelled as well, interpreting interference by their superiors as a slur on the image and status of their heroes. They identified with them, even more so than with the gladiators. This may at first seem rather an odd claim to make, since there are plenty of inscriptions that prove gladiators found great favor with the public, but however popular they may sometimes have been, the bond between charioteers and their fans was even stronger. Spectators could enjoy chariot races far more often, generally on somewhere between twenty and sixty days a year, whereas gladiator games were held only ten to fifteen times annually. Appearances by an individual gladiator were limited to a maximum of between three and five a year, so his chances of becoming a popular favorite were comparatively limited, however bravely he fought. And of course over the head of every gladiator hung the permanent threat of defeat in a life-and-death battle. There was far more chance of that than of a charioteer being killed during a race. Most gladiators died before they reached thirty, after five to fifteen fights, never having had the chance to win a permanent place in the hearts of their fans. By that age most charioteers had participated in hundreds of races. The winners had bought their freedom, made a great deal of money, moved into beautiful houses, and become idolized by their supporters. They did what their fans expected of them: they flaunted their victories, paraded through the streets, surrounded themselves with faithful entourages, were adored by girls and women (married or otherwise), and bought large estates. Only a small number of gladiators had achieved an equivalent status by the time they reached thirty.

After their career ended, charioteers had an opportunity to withdraw from the racetrack for good, but few did so. Most could not live without the applause of the arena and remained connected with the stable in one way or another, as trainers or advisers. The most successful drivers joined the leadership of their stables, acting as sporting directors of a kind, although not in the role of overall boss. Until the third century that position was reserved for people with a financial background, often prominent members of the knightly class.

CHAPTER 7

The Spectators

With a little imagination, the Circus Maximus can be thought of as Rome in microcosm. All ranks and classes were represented, from the emperor to the humblest of proletarians, freedmen, and slaves, all united in their fascination for chariot races. In the first two centuries of the imperial era, Rome had around a million inhabitants. If we stick to the lowest estimate of spectator capacity at the Circus Maximus, 150,000,[1] on a major race day around a seventh of the population of Rome passed through the gates. If we multiply that by twenty, the minimum number of days on which chariot races were organized at the start of the imperial period, it is clear that annually around 3 million people might attend the races. Later the attractions of the Circus Maximus became even greater. In the fourth century there were as many as sixty days a year on which chariot races were held. If all the seats were taken, this would amount to a total visitor number of 9 million, which demonstrates once again the degree to which chariot racing dominated Roman life.

Once the stadium had filled, the dignitaries arrived and made their way to their luxurious seats. The entrance of the emperor was a special event. All the spectators stood up to cheer him and his family as he took his place in his loge. The applause might last a very long time. Martial tells us that the doubtless carefully orchestrated cheers for Emperor Domitian once went on so long that the first four races of the morning program passed unnoticed.[2] Of course there is a degree of poetic license here, but it indicates how much store the emperors set by this applause. During the races the crowd repeatedly struck up chants for the emperor in his loge. Slogans such as "Good luck, emperor, father of the fatherland," "May the gods defend you," and "Rejoice everyone, Rome is safe, for the emperor is safe" echoed around the stands. The emperor could hear from the intensity of the cheering how much affection the people had for him. An emperor who had stayed away from the Circus Maximus on too many race days would have the point firmly brought home to him by the crowd.

By the beginning of the imperial era ordinary people had lost virtually all their political influence. They could communicate with the emperor only in the Circus Maximus, the Colosseum, or the Theater of Marcellus, and the mood might change radically if a crowd that had come to watch the races suddenly turned directly to the emperor, demanding that he reverse a decision only to be rebuffed. The consequences could be serious. Even an emperor who maintained a good relationship with the people of the city ran the risk of facing protests that might lead to riots. Most emperors were aware of this and reacted positively to requests from the people. If they were embarrassed by heckling from the stands and could not decide what to do, they might refuse to give a direct answer or perhaps leave the response to a herald.

Even Commodus (180–92), who although not a particularly tactful emperor was usually acutely aware of the feelings of the people, avoided confrontations with dissatisfied spectators. One day, when he was not present in person at the Circus Maximus, the spectators made known with loud chanting that Commodus must rid himself of Cleander, the prefect of the Praetorian Guard, whom they held responsible for the prevailing shortage of food. Their anger was not spontaneous; Cassius Dio claims it was carefully orchestrated. "It was a race day and the horses were standing ready at the starting line for the seventh race, when suddenly a great host of children ran out onto the racetrack, led by a tall girl who looked fearsome and of whom it was thought, based on all that happened next, that she was a goddess. The children sang in unison many bitter words. The people joined in and shrieked the worst profanities imaginable across the arena. Finally they stood up out of their seats and left the circus to go looking for Commodus (who was in the Quintilian suburb). They wished him every blessing, but they cursed Cleander."[3] Commodus let the people have their way and ordered Cleander's beheading, even though he knew Cleander was not to blame for the inadequate supply of grain but rather the prefect in charge, Papirius Dionysius.

Caligula, in contrast, did enter into open conflict with the crowd, with dire consequences. In the Circus Maximus in 41 he was given to understand that he had acted unjustly in raising taxes. Flavius Josephus, a historian who in *Antiquities of the Jews* throws a great deal of light on Emperor Caligula's final months, describes the confrontation between crowd and emperor that provoked Caligula's murder:

> At that time there were chariot races. This spectator sport is extraordinarily popular among the Romans. Enthusiastically they gather in great throngs at the racetrack, and once they are assembled they make known to the emperor their desires concerning the subjects to which they want to call his attention. Emperors who take the view that such requests cannot be denied know they are assured of the people's good will. They made a passionate appeal to Gaius [Caligula] to lower taxes and reduce the financial burdens on them a little. But he refused to discuss any such thing. When they started shouting even louder he sent soldiers among them, who moved in all directions with orders to arrest the protesters, bring them forward, and kill them there and then. Those were the orders he gave. The soldiers charged with carrying them out did as they were told. Very many people were put to death. The people saw it, held back, and stopped protesting, since they saw with their own eyes that campaigning for tax relief incurred the death penalty. For Chaerea this was an extra stimulus to devise a plot to put an end to the way Gaius was carrying on like a beast in his dealings with the people. Often at the entry of the emperors he had been at the point of acting on his plans, but he had always decided against it after a little contemplation. That he wanted to kill Gaius was certain, he had no doubts about that, but he continued to wait for an appropriate moment, since he did not want to take any action that might prove fruitless but rather to make sure his plans would succeed.[4]

Caligula had called down his fate upon himself. He ought to have known that for ordinary spectators the Circus Maximus was more than just a stadium. It was a safety valve, a place where they could air their grievances. Caligula seriously misjudged the situation, perhaps because he thought the supporters' groups would not act in concert. Blues joining forces with Greens? That could never happen, he must have thought. But he was wrong, and for him the results were disastrous.

Supporters' Groups Attached to the Racing Stables

The spectators came mainly to see the races, of course. The fact that they were in close proximity to the emperor was a bonus, but their real purpose in coming was to be there in person to see their favorite drivers triumph. Few watched the races with the astonished gaze of Ovid (see chapter 5); the vast majority were there as members of one of the supporters' groups attached to the four racing stables, fervently hoping that their stable would carry off the greatest number of prizes. A supporters' group, like its stable, was called a *factio*. In the stands you could see exactly who belonged to which. Sporting the green, blue, red, or white shirts of their factions, people chanted the names of their heroes and voiced their hatred of charioteers for the other three stables in ear-splitting shrieks. Under Domitian there had been six factions for a short time, but the two new racing stables, the Golds and the Purples, were unable to hold their own and disappeared from the scene after Domitian died. The remaining four factions were in existence throughout antiquity, but the Reds and Whites had smaller memberships than the Greens and Blues, eventually becoming what we would call "satellite clubs." The Whites had a cooperative relationship with the Blues, the Reds with the Greens, although occasionally the Whites and the Greens worked together, as did the Blues and the Reds.

An interesting question, but one that a lack of reliable information makes impossible to answer with any confidence, is why a person would become a supporter of one faction rather than another. It has been suggested that the choice was dictated by the district or street in which the supporter lived, in other words that there were true-Blue and true-Green parts of town. This is one possibility, just as we cannot rule out the idea that a supporter's trade or profession played a role in his choice. Although nothing is said about it in the sources, I can well imagine that in a given district members of a trade association for artisans in the same line of work (*collegium*), who regularly saw each other at parties, funerals, and services of worship for their association's tutelary

A charioteer for the Blues, portrayed in his traditional outfit. (Photograph by Jastrow)

deity, went to the Circus Maximus together and sat next to each other on seats rented by that trade association to cheer on the same charioteering stars. It is possible to envision a situation in which coppersmiths were fans of the Greens while carpenters supported the Blues.

For a number of groups in Roman society this rationale does not hold water, however. Senators and knights were guided in their choice mainly by sympathies dictated by tradition, or in some cases by the political climate, by an emperor's preference for a specific faction. Under capricious emperors who openly expressed their love for one particular stable, senators would need to be extremely loyal supporters to find the courage to cheer drivers wearing anything other than the emperor's preferred color.

In many families there was no other topic of conversation in the days leading up to the races. Love for a racing stable might be taken to extremes; some people hardly ever missed a race day in the circus and at other times were regularly to be found at their stable's training complex. On the street and at public events they engaged in ferocious verbal exchanges with followers of other factions, and these sometimes degenerated into shouting matches or fights. Only rarely did brawls turn into actual riots, since the Praetorian Guard and the special city cohorts stayed on top of any trouble and intervened at an early stage should disturbances arise.

There was no holding back some supporters. Their fanaticism for their factions was so great that they identified with their heroes, called themselves Scorpus, Musclosus, or Diocles, and even imitated their mannerisms. Before the races began, they discussed the tactics their favorite drivers ought to employ, and afterward they commented outspokenly on how the races had gone. Dressed in the colors of their racing stables, they were instantly identifiable, and chance passersby would do well to refrain from making any critical remarks about them or their charioteers.

Some fans lost touch with reality completely and tried to influence the races through magical practices. In the light of comparable scenes today in southern countries, where Catholic priests bless football players' boots and racing cyclists' bicycles, it does not seem particularly odd that they sought the support of the gods and prayed to them to assist their heroes in the struggle. More curious is their habit of writing the names of horses and drivers for other factions on curse tablets, with appeals to the gods and the demons of the underworld to bring their opponents to rack and ruin. Several of these tablets have survived in charioteers' graves. They demonstrate that an unconditional love for one's own faction would be accompanied by an irrational hatred of the opposition.

The most fiercely formulated curses come from North Africa, where the supporters were divided into the same four factions and inspired by a fanaticism much like that of supporters in Rome. A tablet found in Hadrumetum with a text written by a Blue or a Red is a vivid example:

"I adjure you, demon whoever you are, and I demand of you from this hour, from this day, from this moment, that you torture and kill the horses of the Greens and Whites and that you kill in a crash their drivers Clarus, Felix, Primulus, and Romanus and leave not a breath in their bodies."[5] Even more outspoken and detailed is the following text from a curse tablet found in Carthage. The writer invokes an unknown person, someone who died young and whose name he apparently does not know, using various epithets:

> I call upon you, spirit of an untimely deceased, whoever you are,
> I call upon you by your almighty names SALBATHBAL AUTHGERO-
> TABAL BASUTHATEO ALEO SAMABETHOR. . . . Bind up the horses
> whose names and likenesses I hereby confide in you. From the
> team of the Reds: Silvanus, Sevator, Lues, Zephyrus, Blandus,
> Imbraius, Dives, Mariscus, Rapidus, Oriens, Arbustus; from the
> Blues: Imminens, Dignus, Linon, Paezon, Chrysaspis, Argutus,
> Diresor, Frugiferus, Euphrates, Sanctus, Aethiops, Praeclarus.
> Restrict their ability to run, their strength, their spirit, their accel-
> eration, their speed. Deny them victory, tangle their feet, obstruct
> them, so that tomorrow morning in the Hippodrome they are
> unable to run or even to walk slowly, to get to the starting stalls
> or make headway on the track. May they fall down, along with
> their drivers, Euprepes, son of Telesphorus, and Gentius and Felix
> and Dionysius the scrapper, and Lamurus. Bind up their hands,
> snatch victory from them, deny them sight, so that they cannot see
> their rivals. Lay hold of them, lift them up out of their chariots,
> pull them out of their chariots and onto the ground, so that they
> fall and are dragged all around the track, especially through the
> turns, and are gravely injured, along with their horses. Do it now,
> quickly.[6]

The production of curse tablets did not end when Christian emperors took control of Rome; they were merely adjusted to suit the new reli-gious climate, as demonstrated by tablets found along the Via Appia, close to the Porta Sebastiano. They date from the late fourth century, when Theodosius and Honorius were emperors, and they use what is obviously a combination of Christian and heathen invocations. Angels are named alongside the demons of the underworld. The job asked of them is the same: to ensure that the cursed charioteer does not win.

> I call on you, holy angels and holy names, to join with the power of the magic spells; bind up Eucherius the charioteer tomorrow in the arena of Rome, trap him, make him fall, cause him injury, destroy him, kill and crush him. Make the starting stalls fail to open properly, stop him from entering the contest fast enough. Stop him from passing the others. Stop him from getting through. Stop him from winning. Stop him from taking the turns properly. Stop him from receiving the accolades. Stop him from getting through to take the lead. Stop him from dashing out from the back of the pack and passing the others and instead make him crash. See to it that he is tethered by your power, that he is crushed, that he is dragged along at the back of the field, both in the early morning races and in all the rest. Now, now. Quickly, quickly.[7]

Some supporters were even prepared to die in order to be united with their heroes. The most striking example of unconditional loyalty is the story of a fan at the burial of Felix, a famous charioteer for the Red faction who had crashed and whose cremation drew a large crowd. The instant the body was laid on the pyre, the supporter threw himself onto the flames next to his dead idol.[8] Followers of the other racing stables, keen to prevent the deceased charioteer from becoming even more famous in death than he had been in life, promptly declared that the unfortunate suicide had acted as he did because he was intoxicated by gaseous emissions from perfume, released by the cremation. But they knew as well as anyone that the fan had been motivated by immeasurable grief and by a longing to be united with his favorite driver in death.

The enthusiasm of the common folk for charioteers who had achieved star status stands in stark contrast to the loyalty toward their supporters, or lack of it, shown by the charioteers themselves. We have no explicit reports of the feelings of drivers for their fans, but from inscriptions, which make clear that many successful charioteers drove for all four stables, it is possible to conclude that they failed to reciprocate the love of their fans in any lasting fashion and that they were primarily

A charioteer in a *quadriga* on a mosaic from Dougga. To his name has been added *Omnia per te* ("Everything through you"). His green helmet and shirt indicate the stable to which he belonged. The names of his horses, Amandus and Frunitus, are also given. (Photograph by Pascal Radigue)

concerned with their own honor and rewards. The disadvantage to a racing stable of their departure and the disappointment of their supporters did not ultimately trouble them much. They wanted to rake in the maximum possible prize money in the ten to fifteen years on average in which they were active, and the color of the stable they raced for did not greatly matter. Their attitude is not so very different from that of today's professional football players, who likewise show little real love for a specific club. They serve the highest bidder and leave before long for a different side, abandoning their old supporters. They are cheered by new fans, sometimes by followers of a local rival who hissed at them only recently. Nobody nowadays is shocked by the transfer of a soccer player from Atletico Madrid to Real Madrid, from AS Roma to Lazio, from Botafogo to Fluminense, even from Glasgow Rangers to Celtic. It takes a little while for supporters to adjust when called upon to cheer for a former "enemy" who is now wearing their own club colors, but as soon as the new acquisition starts to contribute to success on the field, their mistrust evaporates.

In ancient Rome it was no different. The love of supporters for their favorite drivers was severely tested by transfers of top charioteers, but it was unthinkable for any true fan of the Greens to follow his or her beloved charioteer to the Blues. Fans following their favorites to another stable would not have been accepted by the supporters of that stable, and the supporters of their own stable would have threatened to kill them. It would not even have crossed their mind. They felt at home with their faction, which for them was not just a sports club, it was almost a way of life. For those who did more than simply attach themselves to a faction and clap for it, those who became bosses of local branches, for instance, active support was a source of power, and they could briefly forget that in everyday life they were of little or no significance. Their faction gave them a chance to scream away all their frustrations and to achieve some kind of status. It was an outlet for their aggression and other emotions. So each remained loyal to his or her own racing stable and would welcome a new charioteer, having jeered and wished him dead only a little while earlier, when he was a driver for the opposition.

Intellectuals' Writings about Chariot Racing

The loyalty displayed by supporters was not seen by everyone in a positive light. In a letter to his friend Calvisius, Pliny the Younger makes perfectly clear what he thinks of the love of the fans for their club colors. His letter expresses downright incomprehension and contempt. After explaining that he has absolutely no interest in the circus shows—they hold no appeal for him, having neither novelty nor variety—he continues in a facetious tone:

> It amazes me to see thousands and thousands of grown up people behaving like children. All they want to do is to watch the horses galloping and the men standing in the chariots, and they do so over and over again. It might be understandable if it were the speed of the horses or the skill of the charioteers that attracted

them, but really all they're interested in is a color. That's what they support, that's what captivates them. Just imagine if all the charioteers, halfway through a race, exchanged colors. I'm certain the fans would withdraw their support and immediately drop the charioteers and horses whose names they'd been shouting across the arena and whom they can identify from a long way off. The overpowering influence of one cheap tunic is as enormous as that, and not only on the vulgar herd but on many respectable men.[9]

Pliny makes it sound as if the supporters were in love merely with the color of a shirt, but this indicates that he understood little about fanaticism among fans. Like many other intellectuals, he made no attempt to comprehend the emotions of the crowds in the stands, and he refused to acknowledge that they became instantly heartbroken and suffered real pain if one of their favorite charioteers was defeated. He could not comprehend their great affection for the drivers of their factions or why they said of themselves not "I'm for the Greens" but "I'm a Green." Pliny and those of like mind reasoned purely from their own perspective. With deep-rooted prejudice they contrasted their own intellectual activities with the concerns of the supporters massed around the racetrack.

Remarkably, three hundred years later church father Augustine did show some understanding for the behavior of fans at the Circus Maximus. Although he too was an outsider who felt little affinity for the phenomenon of chariot racing, his comments reveal that he well understood the emotions that governed supporters. He even used their fanaticism, their unconditional, steadfast love for their favorite drivers, in a sermon, presenting it as a good example to his Christian brothers and sisters. The heathen fans were completely absorbed by this love of theirs, forgetting everything else until they no longer knew who or where they were, and in a similar way the faithful must set everything else aside and rely totally, in love and hope, on the one true God.[10]

The historian Tacitus was no less reluctant than his friend Pliny the Younger to empathize with the fans' behavior. He deplored the fact that every child acquired a passion for the theater, gladiator fights, and chariot races on its mother's knee.[11] Nero's desire to perform as a charioteer—he argued that he was acting in the tradition of his ancestors—was incomprehensible to Tacitus, who speaks of a scandalous intention[12] and makes it seem as if others wholeheartedly endorse his criticism. In describing how Subrius Flavus, an officer of the Praetorian Guard, defended before Nero his involvement in a coup, he puts the following words into his mouth: "I hated you. Yet in your army there was not one soldier more loyal than I, as long as you were worthy of the people's love. I began to hate you when you became the murderer of your mother and your wife and revealed yourself to be a charioteer, a play actor, and a firesetter."[13] Tacitus agreed with those who said that people from the better circles should strive after higher goals and not concern themselves with chariot races, since such events only distracted them from the finer things in life, the arts that really counted: literature and philosophy. How could charioteers, those infamous characters, teach the people anything of value? Theirs was an entertainment from which intellectuals should distance themselves.

The pronouncements of Pliny and Tacitus might give the impression that they never saw the inside of the Circus Maximus, but a brief remark in a letter from Pliny to a man called Maximus reveals that Tacitus, at least, had certainly been there.[14] It seems his intellectual disdain for the chariot races was not so profound as to make the stands around the racetrack forbidden territory to him. He was no doubt far from the only aristocrat whose low opinion of chariot racing was less deeply rooted than he was willing to admit. In truth such contempt was probably aimed primarily at those who visited the circus regularly: the plebeians.

The attitude of Stoic philosopher Seneca tends to confirm that this kind of hostility was really targeted at ordinary people as such. He barely mentions chariot racing and says little about charioteers. For him the racing is all about the environment, the craze, the frenzy, the heaving circus with its thousands of spectators casting off all restraint, no longer in control of their emotions. They represent the masses, people miles removed from him. The fact that chariot races appeal to the common herd is enough in itself to make them a far from elevating spectacle. Surely intellectuals could never expose themselves to that crowd. They should have other, higher aims in view.

The only authors who do have some understanding of the world of the Circus Maximus are those already quoted: Martial and Juvenal.

Their comments reveal that they knew the circus at first hand, and they speak in favor of it quite openly. Martial refers to horses and drivers by name; he writes about the supporters' groups, the colors, and the racing stables. One problem here is that with Martial it is always hard to tell when he is expressing his own opinions and when he is voicing the thoughts of ordinary people themselves. He sounds negative only when he brings up the subject of the earnings of the most successful charioteers. He cannot resist expressing his disapproval of their extravagant prizes.

Juvenal too probably had firsthand experience of the Circus Maximus. He names horses and drivers but gives no details about how the races went or which particular charioteering skills were on show. He cannot have been a regular visitor, since in his *Satires* he writes quite disapprovingly about chariot races, making a firm connection between them and the passions of the common folk.[15] His famous and much cited maxim about "bread and circuses," which sums up his negative view of ordinary people, is illustrative of his outlook.[16]

In fact, the appeal of the chariot races to countless Romans is probably the most important reason that the writers of antiquity say so little about them. They did not want to be accused of enthusiasm for the same form of entertainment that was enjoyed by the masses. There were only two ways they could avert this kind of suspicion: by ignoring the chariot races altogether or by limiting themselves to oblique remarks about the baleful influence of the circus on ordinary folk. Sometimes authors could not resist writing about the races, but they generally chose their words with such attention to "political correctness" that the elite would have few grounds on which to reproach them.

In his passage about club colors, Pliny could not ignore the fact that there were senators who thought differently, indeed more positively, about chariot racing. With obvious reluctance he had to admit that those contemptible tunics worn by the charioteers captivated not only the rabble but some very prominent figures—Marcus Cornelius Fronto, for example. This senator, who had schooled emperors Marcus Aurelius and Lucius Verus in the art of rhetoric, wrote in a letter that a problem with his hand one day had made it impossible for him to annotate a manuscript he had been asked to comment on, but it had not deterred him from visiting the circus. The ailment was playing up painfully, yet he had once more been gripped by the thrill of the racetrack.[17] He would not have been alone, although the number of senators who openly admitted to such enthusiasm was small.

Betting on the Contests

Another reason that intellectuals were less than keen to write about the Circus Maximus was that betting on the outcome was common, both prior to and during the races. All sectors of the population participated. Their bets varied, but not the zeal with which they placed them. Betting on the races or on other contests such as games of dice was in bad odor with the elite, since a wise person was supposed to avoid taking blind risks. Gamblers were regarded as individuals who had no control over their affairs, who surrendered themselves to folly with unpredictable consequences. Gambling was a threat to the integrity of a person's character, and it led to addiction. Those who placed bets often had other vices, and the word *aleator* (gambler) was used as a term of abuse along with other negative epithets like "adulterer" and "drunkard." Status was relevant here as well. Because the common people were not expected to live thoughtful, rational lives, it was among their ranks, so people felt, that gamblers were most likely to be found.

Of course everyone in Rome knew that holders of high office placed bets just as fanatically as ordinary Romans and that past emperors had included several notorious gamblers and dice players. Augustus, who took pride in having restored the old norms and values, made no secret of the fact that he regularly played dice for high stakes.[18] Caligula was an avid gambler, too; he even failed to turn up on the day of his sister Drusilla's funeral, so absorbed had he become in games of dice.[19] Claudius must really have gone too far in the eyes of more conventional aristocrats, since not only was he a dedicated dice player but he wrote a book about it. Even while he was traveling, he could not keep his hands off the dice.[20] Seneca regarded Claudius's addiction as so extreme that as a punishment he wished upon him an eternal game of dice with a bottomless cup.[21] Nero, Vitellius, Domitian, Lucius Verus, Commodus, and Didius Julianus were among the other emperors who threw themselves into dice playing with wild abandon.[22] All of them, with the possible exception of Augustus, had a great fondness for chariot racing as well, and so it is safe to assume that they combined their two passions and bet large sums on the outcome of the races.

Gladiator fights and chariot races lent themselves particularly well to gambling, since gamblers could use known facts about the competing parties to help them decide how high their stake should be. Regular visitors to the Colosseum knew the background of every gladiator who was due to perform. Posters and program booklets told them who would be fighting whom in the arena, and they could decide how much to bet accordingly, although these cool calculations of chance would be balanced by a preference for one particular type of fighter in a contest. It was rare for two gladiators to confront each other with exactly the same weapons. Gladiator bosses usually selected combatants with contrasting equipment. A follower of the fighters with small shields, the *parmularii*, would not readily put his money on a gladiator of the type who fought with large shields, the *scutarii*. Nevertheless, if a favorite fighter stepped into the arena against a renowned opponent likely to be stronger than he was, reason would often have prevailed over emotion, and the bet would have been placed on the likely winner.

The volume of betting on chariot races, whether at home, in the street, or at the Circus Maximus, must have been far greater still. The crowd was more numerous, shows were held more often, and the charioteers and horses, each performing more frequently than any gladiator, held few potential surprises for experienced gamblers. Everyone placing a bet in the Circus Maximus knew how many victories his chosen charioteer had to his name, the color of his racing stable, and which particular horses he drove.

Irrational arguments and sentiment played their part, too. For days before the charioteering began, astrologers were consulted and asked to predict the outcome of races by studying the stars. A Byzantine manuscript from the thirteenth century, which describes practices that go back to the Roman imperial era, includes the following text: "You should know that the moon helps the Greens, the sun the Reds, and Saturn and Venus the Blues. So if the sun conjuncts Venus precisely at the moment the Blues shoot forward in the race, they will achieve victory. If the sun conjuncts Mars, it is the Greens who will triumph. Because Mars assists them. And if Jupiter is directly overhead, then the Blues are sure to win, especially if the moon is deprived of light at that moment."[23] This pronouncement was made by a professional astrologer in a study into the influence of astrologers on supporters in Rome and Constantinople in the distant past. The writer does not describe the extent of their power or say whether they were consulted regularly, or even whether they were paid for their services, but when we consider the curse tablets in which demons of the underworld were exhorted to annihilate the drivers of all other parties, it does not seem at all strange that keen gamblers among the supporters, longing for good results, turned their eyes to the heavens, to the stars and the planets, and to the gods who were so inextricably associated with them.

Despite the popularity of betting on chariot races, it seems unlikely that any large betting shops existed. We have no reports of anything of the kind, although of course we cannot exclude the possibility that this is simply due to the low opinion many aristocrats had of all things connected with gambling. There were few, if any, firm rules governing bets, which were made informally between random individuals, at home, in bars, in the street, and in the circus. Sometimes a shrewd businessman would take the initiative, coordinating the bets and acting as a bookmaker. It may seem rather odd to us, but it was perfectly natural from the Romans' point of view that fewer bets would be placed on individual drivers and horses than on racing stables. The choice was between the Greens, the Blues, the Reds, and the Whites, and which particular chariot won for its stable was of secondary importance. By betting on the Blue or the Green racing stable, the two known to have the best drivers and horses, you were more likely to win than by betting on the Reds or the Whites, but the odds, the ratio between money put down and winnings paid out, made up for this. With the Greens and the Blues you could win a maximum of double the amount wagered; with the Whites and the Reds six times the sum would not have been unusual. If a top charioteer was racing for one of the two minor stables, however, this gap closed right up. Diocles, who raced successfully for the Reds for a long time, made his small stable suddenly the favorite. It went to the top of the bookies' lists, and so the amounts paid out in individual winnings were lower.

It seems very likely that people could bet on a combination of racing stables. In the imperial era, mention is repeatedly made of a merger of the Blues with the Reds and the Greens with the Whites. The question as to why they performed together in a number of races can in my view be answered only if we accept that people were able to bet on such "combinations." Instead of four, the gambler now had only two options, which made for increased eagerness among those with few resources, who would otherwise be unable to bet at all. They needed to calculate the odds for only two possible outcomes. For example, a bookmaker could offer bets on a favorite team of Blues and Reds at 1:2 and on the other team at 2:1, thereby creating a pool of 100 percent with a stake of two sestertii for the Reds or the Blues and one sestertius for the Greens or the Whites.[24] For the leaders of the small racing stables, this kind of cooperation offered a major advantage in that it increased their chances of success in the races. They would probably take a share of the prize money even if the winner was not from their stable. So gambling contributed to the survival of the racing stables.

Spectators who had placed bets must sometimes have panicked as they watched their favorite drivers and horses being outpaced and their stakes evaporating. Perhaps it was more painful still for people who could not be present at the races in person and had placed substantial bets through trusted intermediaries. They had to wait for quite some time, especially if they lived a long distance away, to hear the results of a race. A certain Caecina from Volaterrae, two hundred kilometers to the north of Rome, found the wait unbearable and thought of a way around it, knowing his gambling fellow citizens would be longing to hear the results. Pliny the Elder claims Caecina took a swallow (perhaps he means a homing pigeon) to the races in a basket.[25] As soon as the race on which his fellow townspeople had gambled was over, he painted one of the bird's wings in the winning color and freed it. The swallow flew away, and within hours it was able to inform the gamblers of the result, long before the news would otherwise have reached them.

Riots?

The ferocity shown by supporters' groups toward each other will surprise no one. Spectators sat mixed together, but the hard core of the four factions had their own seats and made a considerable noise. They stamped their feet, clapped their hands, shouted the names of their

A relief on a panel from a sarcophagus, depicting a chariot race. The drivers have been replaced by little cupids, which do not look at all like real charioteers. (Photograph by Georges Jansoone)

favorite charioteers, and tried to shout down the followers of the other stables. In the pandemonium of the Circus Maximus, large groups must surely have got out of hand fairly regularly, with outbreaks of serious violence. But questions as to what form this violence took inside and outside the circus are not dealt with by the authors of the ancient world. They suggest it could be turbulent up in the stands, but they do not go into detail. There are no stories about supporters rioting, about vandalism or fighting, or about dead or wounded spectators.

It is therefore difficult to say whether there were any major riots in the first two centuries of the imperial era. Most historians follow Alan Cameron in his standard work *Circus Factions* in thinking that the violence around the racetrack was not particularly serious in this period. According to Cameron, there was no real fighting between supporters of the four factions, only arguments that arose from a sense of impotence among individuals or groups of supporters, who then lost their self-control out of frustration and disappointment.[26] Only later in antiquity and in the Byzantine period did anything occur that could be described as organized mass violence among supporters. It is undeniable that from the fourth century onward the factions were seen in a more political light than in the first three centuries AD (see chapter 8), but this does not mean we should assume that large groups of fans had rarely, if ever, been known to misbehave before.

As we have seen, all over the Roman Empire curse tablets have been found on which fanatical supporters wish upon the drivers of the other racing stables the worst fates imaginable. It would surely be odd if the fury and hatred expressed in these texts toward individual opponents, racing stables as a whole, and crowds of opposition supporters did not sometimes translate into violent behavior in the stands. Whether or not this led to large-scale confrontations, the fact remains that the conditions for such an outcome were present. In my view the apolitical character of Roman plebeians is too often given as a reason that they did not become an organized force and use violence to back up their demands. The poet Juvenal observed that a defeat for the Greens could deeply distress supporters, and he compares their dejection to the despondency that overcame Rome after its defeat at Cannae by the Carthaginians in 216 BC,[27] but he does not take this point any further. He says nothing about how they dealt with their disappointment.

It is clear that Roman audiences could kick up a storm and did not shrink from rioting. We need only to look at the theater, where people lost control of themselves during stage shows and expressed their dissatisfaction through violence. Sometimes it was confined to minor scuffles, sometimes there were brawls that continued outside the theater. The authorities were often forced to intervene. Descriptions of the behavior of theater audiences seem far removed from accounts that point to relatively restrained conduct by supporters in the Circus Maximus. It seems almost as if these were two different worlds, whereas in fact the same ordinary people went to watch both forms of popular entertainment.

No one in Ancient Rome was surprised that theater audiences regularly turned into a rabble, with plays prompting unrestrained aggression in spectators. To some extent this is attributable to the subjects dealt with in works for the stage, which quite often portrayed recent events with highly emotional content. The actors, insignificant members of Roman society in social, legal, and political terms, heightened the effect by giving their plays a political twist, exciting audiences and inciting aggressive behavior. The actors, frustrated in everyday life, felt themselves lord and master on stage and "took revenge" by pandering to feelings of dissatisfaction among the common folk, who then completely let themselves go, just as the leading actors intended them to.

Sometimes the situation deteriorated, and audiences engaged in fist-fights both with each other and with the forces sent to restore order. After the theater was cleared, they would continue fighting outside, vandalizing the surrounding area until the police put a stop to that, too. The Roman elite abhorred the popular theater and all the peripheral phenomena associated with it.

Police units of the Praetorian Guard and the city cohorts, who were responsible for upholding law and order, often watched helplessly as the interplay between actors and audiences led to explosions of violence. The government did not always have a ready-made solution. Peace was usually restored after a while, but often the tension remained palpable, and there was a risk the actors might prompt a resumption of violence. The ultimate response from the authorities was to punish the actors severely. They would be charged with posing a threat to public order and safety and with serving up plays that had a pernicious influence on public morals. Sometimes, if all other measures had proven ineffective, they were banned from the city. Even Nero, not exactly a paragon of decency, felt compelled at one point to crack down on actors and their most fanatical followers, although he did so only after allowing the situation to get out of hand.

Given that disturbances among theater audiences were so common, it is strange that the authors of antiquity, in the brief references they make to shows in the Circus Maximus, seem to suggest that the crowds and the main players behaved very differently there. It is almost as if those 150,000 spectators sat in disciplined rows to watch the chariot races and kept their emotions completely under control. I feel forced to question the impression that arises from these ancient writings, since to me it is barely conceivable that in the seething Circus Maximus feelings never flared up. We need only think of today's football stadiums to realize where bottled-up emotions and outbursts of rage can lead. I do not have in mind hooligans who go to the stadium with the premeditated intention of raising hell but loyal fans who live and suffer along with their favorite stars and occasionally throw off all restraint. It would surely be very strange if ancient Rome were any different, if the crowds there summoned so much self-control that they never turned into a mob. Supporters of the Greens or the Blues who identified with their heroes in the arena must have been driven to despair at regular intervals by crashes, by seeing their heroes defeated right at the finishing line, and by provocative chants from other groups of supporters. Situations must surely have arisen in which they could no longer contain themselves and expressed their frustration in violence.

In that case, why do Roman authors never mention it? Why do they tell us the theaters were cleared and actors banished from the city but say nothing about disturbances in the Circus Maximus? Are we to conclude that there were no riots or at least none so serious that the authors considered them worth writing about? That would be too simple an explanation. Even in our own day very few literary authors report directly on football matches and the disturbances that occur at them. If they throw any light on such events at all, they do so in columns, essays, letters to the editors of newspapers and magazines, or in literary periodicals, in the form of detached analysis, not in factual reports describing the extent of the violence and specifying the number of casualties. In Roman literature, too, remarks about the chariot races and all that went with them appear almost exclusively in works written for some other purpose. There are no direct references to the friction and commotion of a race day at the Circus Maximus.

It would be intriguing to be able to study Roman newspaper reports of riots, but unfortunately no newspapers have come down to us, and it is far from certain the Romans had anything of the kind. Reports of community events were written on white plaster tablets that have since been lost. The closest to our newspapers were the *acta diurna*, daily bulletins introduced by Caesar and used by the emperors as an ideal medium for publicizing news about "the emperor and society." Emperors would not have allowed negative reports about the racetrack or anything else that displeased them to be included. For an emperor to admit he was incapable of keeping order would have been to label himself impotent, thereby seriously damaging his image as "patron of all."

The fact that literary sources make little mention of circus riots has to do above all with the world writers moved in. Many critics did not have any real understanding of chariot racing and made little secret of the fact, but they also realized that many in their own circles saw things quite differently. They knew they were free to write negative things about the popular theater because it was not authentically Roman and it challenged many traditional virtues. Actors were seen as feeble, effeminate individuals who led people away from the straight path of virtue with their provocative performances. Their success was ephemeral. When they were chased out of town, protests from their fans were vehement but short lived. They were quickly forgotten. Writers had to be more careful when it came to damning criticism of chariot races. Charioteers were star athletes who could achieve limitless popularity despite their low social status. They were revered for their daring and dexterity, and, perhaps most important of all, theirs was a sport firmly rooted in Roman society whose origins lay in the activities of the elite in the time of the kings.

Emperors were well aware that they had to proceed with caution when riots broke out in the Circus Maximus. If they used the same policies to quash disturbances as they did to punish impertinent stage actors, they would only succeed in fanning the flames of unrest. A ban on chariot racing would inevitably have led to more riots and perhaps to orchestrated anger among the people, something all Roman emperors were apprehensive about, since they could not rule out the possibility that a frustrated populace would receive moral support from aristocrats who were just as fanatically keen on chariot racing as they were.

An emperor knew that any rioting that broke out in the course of a day at the races was not aimed at him personally but was the result of the way the racing had gone. He too was a follower of one of the racing stables, and so a situation might arise in which he would have to punish violent supporters of his own faction. That would not do his popularity any good. By the same token, measures taken against the fans of other factions were hazardous, since the emperor might find himself accused of bias.

So when disturbances broke out in the Circus Maximus, the emperor faced a dilemma. Should he take action at all, and if so what should he do? He could ignore minor instances of disorder, playing them down to avoid having to act or at least keeping his response to a minimum, or he could take firm measures to sort things out. Although in the first and second centuries imperial authority was usually sufficient to maintain order, meaning there was no need to resort to the same repressive measures as in the theater, situations must regularly have arisen in which emperors had to intervene to put a stop to outbreaks of violence by force. The authors, who often belonged to the emperor's circle of acquaintances, ignored this, on the one hand because they did not think such things worth mentioning and on the other because they wanted to avoid any possibility of reports of disturbances being interpreted as veiled criticism of an emperor who had allowed matters to get out of hand.

To some outsiders who did not belong to the traditional Roman elite, the Circus Maximus was clearly a place where frenzy was unleashed, where spectators lost all self-control. In the early third century, Tertullian, a Christian writer from North Africa and a self-declared opponent of all Roman spectator sports, advised his fellow believers to keep away from the circus because the things that went on there were totally unacceptable:

> Since this madness is forbidden to us as Christians, we stay well away from every show, including those in the circus, where a particular insanity prevails. Just look at the people, how quickly they become enthralled by this spectacle, how completely unrestrained, blind, and agitated they are in their delusion. When the praetor performs his tasks it all goes too slowly for them, their eyes are fixed on the urn he has in his hands, in which they are shaken up together, as it were, along with the lots. Then they wait full of anxious suspense for the starting signal, united by their shrieks, united in their frenzy. You can tell they are mad from their behavior: the *quadrigae* have barely set off before they start reporting on what they have seen. I regard it as a form of blindness. They don't see what's been thrown down, they think it's the starting flag, but in reality it's the figure of the devil flung from the dizzying heights.
>
> And immediately the insanity begins, the frenzy, the vexation, the discord, and all those things that are unbefitting to the priests of peace [i.e., Christians]. Then you hear abuse everywhere, curses not justified by any hatred and encouragements not inspired by any love. What do they aim to achieve with their excitement, if

they can't even keep themselves in hand? Perhaps simply to cease being their own masters. They mourn for the mishaps of strangers and rejoice at the good fortune of others. Whatever they desire and whatever they abominate, it has nothing to do with them. Consequently their love is senseless and their hatred unfounded. Or is it permissible to love without reason and to hate without cause?

God forbids us to hate, even when we have reason for it. He instructs us to love, even to love our enemies. God simply will not tolerate cursing, even when there are grounds for it. He commands us to speak positively about even the most evil-minded person. But what could be more abominable than the circus, where the spectators have no consideration even for the highest officials or their fellow citizens?[28]

Putting Tertullian's Christian bias aside, we are forced to conclude that in the circus an atmosphere prevailed in which the slightest incident could spark hatred, fury, and madness. At some distance from Rome, in provincial towns, writers were less scrupulous and less hesitant about speaking openly of misbehavior and violence in the circus. The most gripping testimony about a crowd that lost control is that of Dio Chrysostom in the second half of the first century AD. To judge by what he wrote, he had experienced chariot racing at close proximity, drinking it in. He is amazed by the fanatical enthusiasm for the races in Alexandria. He writes that the Alexandrians were not simply supporters, they were obsessed with the hippodrome. When they gathered at the racetrack, they behaved as if under the influence of drugs: "They constantly leapt up from their seats, they screamed and yelled, they let fly at each other and from their mouths came the most terrible curses. They flung their clothes at the charioteers and sometimes even left the circus completely naked."[29] Outside the hippodrome they simply carried on. They hit each other with sticks, drew their swords, threw stones, and caused serious damage to property.[30] Although Dio Chrysostom devotes only a few lines to the "sickness" of the Alexandrians, I think his depiction of a crowd worked up into a frenzy comes closer to the reality than do the aloof observations of Roman authors. His report has a familiar ring. It would not be out of place in the sports section of a newspaper today.

Emperor and Faction

We have already noted that emperors were frequently to be found in the Circus Maximus. Most did not sit there as neutral spectators but as fans of a faction. They openly demonstrated their support outside the racetrack as well, and so spectators knew exactly how far they could go without turning the emperor against them. Emperors almost always favored the Blues or the Greens, hardly ever the Reds or the Whites. "Good" emperors had some sense of moderation; "bad" emperors did not know when to stop, going so far as to interfere with the races personally to influence the outcome. A few even climbed into a racing chariot and took part in races themselves.

The first emperor, Augustus, was in many respects an enigmatic figure, and it is difficult to know how great his enthusiasm for the chariot races really was. Suetonius says of him:

> He himself generally viewed the games at the Circus Maximus from the dining room of a friend or a freed man, sometimes from the emperor's loge, where he would sit in the company of his wife and children. For hours at a time, sometimes for whole days, he absented himself from the games, having first offered his apologies and appointed people to preside in his place. When he was present, he did not busy himself with other things, perhaps so as not to be exposed to the sort of remarks people made about his father Caesar, as he remembered it, complaining about the way Caesar spent his time at the shows reading and answering letters and petitions, and perhaps also because of his own fascination for the games and the pleasure they gave him.[31]

His successor, Tiberius (14–37), was rarely to be found in the Circus Maximus. He did not like major spectacles and made no secret of the fact. Caligula (37–41), however, who succeeded him, was a true devotee; in fact, it would not be unfair to say that his feelings about the races were those of absurd infatuation and that he indulged in all the deeply unattractive practices that accompany such a phenomenon. There was little harm in his habit of regularly dining and spending the night in the Greens' stables, but the fact that once, at a victory party, he made the charioteer Eutychus a gift on the spot of the astronomical sum of twenty million sestertii is a little harder to take. That he was not above having his rivals' horses and drivers killed simply adds to the evidence of his base character.

His love for a horse called Incitatus could safely be described as pathological. Once, on the day before the races began, he told soldiers near the stable in which the horse was resting to make sure everyone was absolutely silent so that its sleep would not be disturbed. To ensure it optimal care he provided not only a marble stable, an ivory feeding bowl, purple horsecloths, and strings of pearls but a house, servants, and household goods so that the horse would be able to entertain appropriately any guests invited to a banquet on its behalf. Caligula regularly asked Incitatus to dinner. He would serve the horse grains of barley in a gold feeding bowl and have wine poured into gold cups to drink its health. It is said he even considered appointing Incitatus to the position of consul. Cassius Dio wrote almost two centuries later that he would certainly have done so had he lived long enough.[32]

Lucius Verus (161–69), who died young and was coemperor with Marcus Aurelius, went to comparable extremes more than two centuries later out of love for his favorite horse, Volucer (Flyer). Like Caligula, he was a great fan of the Greens, and he regularly prompted catcalls from the Blues by showering excessive honors on Volucer after yet another victory. The followers of the Greens profited from his enthusiasm, since every time Volucer stepped onto the racetrack the coemperor gave the Green stable money. He personally saw to it that the horse wanted for nothing and even ordered the stable lads to include nuts and wine-quality grapes in Volucer's daily diet. Outside the racetrack his love for the horse assumed grotesque proportions. In his palace he named an enormous crystal goblet after it, and when he traveled, he always had a small picture of the creature with him. When Volucer died, Lucius Verus had a mausoleum built at the top of the Vatican hill.[33]

Different but certainly no less eccentric was the behavior of supporter Nero (54–68). Ever since childhood he had adored the races in the Circus Maximus, a fact that did not please everyone. In his early youth he spoke one day to a couple of fellow pupils about the sorry fate of a charioteer for the Greens who had been dragged along the track by his horses. When he was reprimanded by his teacher, who felt he ought to be discussing more elevated subjects, he responded that he had been referring to Hector, the Trojan hero who was dragged along behind Achilles' chariot.[34] The races always remained his great passion. He was present as often as possible, and he personally saw to it that a day at the Circus Maximus lasted until well into the evening. Perhaps it was the emotions aroused by the chariot races that caused Nero to lose what was left of his self-control when, after a long day in the Circus Maximus, he kicked his heavily pregnant wife, Poppaea Sabina, to death after she criticized him for coming home late.

Nero took the reins himself, training in the Circus Vaticanus. Unconfirmed reports suggest he was following the example of Caligula, who had laid out this arena purely for his own entertainment. Nero's ambition, however, went beyond personal performances closed to the public. He invited many members of his inner circle to attend the "shows" in his private circus. Predictably, all those present praised him to the skies. Tacitus, in whose work this anecdote is to be found, adds cynically that the common people were delighted that the emperor shared their interest in chariot racing.[35]

It is unlikely Nero was a great charioteer. As far as we know, he never took part in an official race in the Circus Maximus, although he did perform on the racetrack at Olympia. During the Olympic Games he jumped in at the deep end by signing up for a race between ten-horse chariots. It was not exactly a success. During the race he was thrown out of his chariot. After being helped back into it by staff who rushed to his aid, he resumed the race but failed to reach the finishing line, as he was unable to keep control of his team. This did not prevent the organizers from declaring him the winner.[36]

Another fan of the Greens was Commodus (180–91), son of Marcus Aurelius. His father, a true Stoic, had a deep aversion to mass popular entertainment and visited the Colosseum and the Circus Maximus only when absolutely obliged to do so, but his son could barely be dragged away. He won a degree of renown as a gladiator and as a hunter in the arena but made no impression at all with his performances as a charioteer. He drove only on moonless nights, well away from the gaze of an inquisitive public. He never took part in races at the Circus Maximus, supposedly regarding it as beneath his dignity. The real reason was probably that he was not particularly good and feared the common

Nero. (Photograph by Jastrow)

people would quickly realize this.[37] When he drove his chariot under cover of darkness, he always wore the shirt of the Greens—his love for that faction was boundless.

Commodus too had a favorite horse, Pertinax (the Persistent), which had won many victories. The name of the horse caused him serious embarrassment on a number of occasions in the last year of his reign. After Pertinax won a race, while the Greens were loudly shouting his name, fans of the other factions yelled, "If only that were true," an allusion to the aspirations of one of the consuls, who was also called

Commodus. (Photograph by Jastrow)

Pertinax. Later that year, when age forced Pertinax to retire from the arena, Commodus had the horse appear there for the last time, with its hooves gilded and its skin painted gold. The people shouted en masse, "It is Pertinax," implying that for Commodus too the time had come to make way for someone else. A few days later he was assassinated, and Pertinax became the new emperor.[38]

Heliogabalus (218–23), the most eccentric of all the emperors from just about every point of view, regarded no means of attracting attention as too ridiculous. Everything had to be bigger and more impressive, and he simply did not care whether it passed muster with those around him. He had an odd way of expressing his passion for chariot racing. Although not blessed with any discernible talent, he insisted on becoming a charioteer. Fearful of proving a huge disappointment, he performed in his own Circus Varianus rather than the Circus Maximus. He drove his laps of the track in the Green tunic, watched by those loyal to him, including his grandmother, his mother, several other women, and a group of senior functionaries including judges and knights, imperial officials, senators, and the city prefect. He copied everything that real charioteers did, asking for gold coins as a winner's bonus and giving the traditional salute to the organizer of the "games" and the followers of his faction.[39] Sometimes he went a step further and arranged for the chariots to be drawn by elephants, camels, dogs, or deer, on a few occasions even by lions and tigers.[40] It did not make him popular. The people regarded his intemperate behavior as yet more evidence of a disturbed personality.

Only two emperors, Vitellius (69) and Caracalla (211–17), openly admitted that they were followers of the Blues. They did not balk at having fans of other factions killed, especially those of their main rivals, the Greens. In 69 Vitellius had only just come to power when he started a real crusade against the Greens. Whenever he heard that something unpleasant had been said about the Blues, he took it as a form of lèse majesté and condemned the detractors to death or captivity. These harsh punishments are particularly remarkable given that considerable doubts exist as to whether his sympathies lay with the Blues all his life. If Suetonius is not mistaken, he was a Green for a while in his youth and during Caligula's reign he assisted the emperor in his attempts to become a good charioteer. It is possible that he was a sincere supporter

Caracalla. (Photograph by iessi; CC-BY–2.0.)

of the Greens in those years, but it seems more likely that he did not want to get on the wrong side of Caligula, whose fits of temper and ungovernable behavior were legendary, and therefore took to behaving like a Green for the time being.[41]

In Caracalla we see a similar hatred of everyone who was not a fan of the Blues. The situation was even more intimidating than under Vitellius, since Caracalla regularly performed in public in the Blue tunic, not just in Rome but on racetracks along the Danube and farther east. He acted like a real charioteer, greeting the crowd from the racetrack with his whip and asking for gold coins when his performance was over. Anyone with the audacity to take the emperor's act less than seriously was risking his or her neck. Once, when the people booed a driver for the Blues who was especially revered by Caracalla, several paid with their lives.[42] His irrational rage toward the Greens was fueled in part by his hatred of his brother Geta, a fanatical follower of that faction. He killed his brother with his own hands, and the charioteers Geta had adored were made to pay too. They were slaughtered along with several gladiators, musicians, and actors.

None of the fanatical emperors mentioned here enjoyed a good reputation; they all fall under the heading of "bad emperors." "Good emperors," such as Trajan, Hadrian, and Antoninus Pius, behaved far more cautiously, attending the chariot races without making any personal preference for either stable too obvious. We cannot exclude the possibility that the authors of antiquity exaggerated the reprehensible habits of "bad emperors." It is worth noting in this context that the philosopher-emperor Marcus Aurelius said of himself that he had never been a supporter of either the Greens or the Blues,[43] thereby conforming to the ideal image of a good emperor as *pater patriae*, "father of the fatherland." An overly blatant expression of support for one or other racing stable would have been incompatible with this ideal.

CHAPTER 8

Changes around
the Racetrack

Until 235 all Roman emperors, with the exception of Macrinus, had previously been senators. The city of Rome and Roman traditions were central to the way they conducted themselves. Good emperors knew exactly how far they could go; bad emperors found out after a while that overstepping the boundaries could have disastrous consequences. The ascent to the throne in 235 of Maximinus the Thracian, a soldier who had none of the traditional aristocratic ties with Rome, represented a break with the past. He and a number of his successors had risen to greatness through the army, and they had that army to thank for their seizure of power. Their ties with Rome, both with the Senate and with the townsfolk, were weak; for them Rome was no more than an idea. Some had never even laid eyes on the capital of the Roman Empire and believed that if they could control their own native regions the rest of the empire would follow automatically. Those few subsequent emperors who did have a senatorial background were not in a position to put their stamp on the municipal government in their short reigns or to breathe new life into the old norms and values. Rome sank into despair. In the city the realization gradually dawned that the magnificent past had come to an end.

For the inhabitants of Rome the crisis of the third century had huge consequences. Without overdramatizing the economic decline of the empire and the power vacuum at the top, we can say at the very least that the people of Rome, who had felt secure for so long under the protection of powerful emperors, were being made to pay the price for a new political and economic instability. Support in the form of consistent supplies of grain, oil, and wine was cut back, and this naturally put the relationship between the emperor and his people under strain. It had seemed only natural over the previous two centuries for the people to obey their emperor, but that era had ended. No longer assured of material assistance, they began to behave with less discipline. The reaction of the emperors was predictable. Those among them who cared little for Rome left the people to their fate, whereas emperors who had spent a great deal of time in the city endeavored to create the impression that Rome was still the center of a great empire and that they would personally safeguard the interests of ordinary residents. Gladiator fights and chariot races were intended to reinforce this impression, but no matter how spectacular the shows were, they could not disguise the fact that Rome was losing ground to other large cities of the empire.

In 284, after fifty years of political instability, Diocletian came to power, one of the more decisive of Rome's emperors. He believed the empire had grown too big to be ruled by one man, so he transferred governmental authority to four new capital cities, Nicomedia, Sirmium, Milan, and Trier, seats of power for himself, his coemperor, and two junior coemperors. Rome had ceased, for the time being, to be the capital of the empire. Each of these administrative centers needed a suitable circus, and in the early fourth century the four new residences acquired large racetracks, sited directly adjacent to their imperial palaces so that the emperor, coemperor, or junior coemperor could command an audience virtually from the balcony of his throne room. The laying out of these new racetracks was more than merely a show of power; it represented a new phase in the long history of the Roman chariot races, which now became firmly established in the East.

To explain the late introduction of the Roman variant of chariot racing in the eastern part of the empire, we need look no further than the Greek version, which was deeply rooted all across the region. As we have seen, chariot races were organized in Greece from the eighth century BC onward, but in contrast to Rome, where they became a stand-alone form of popular entertainment, they remain linked to major festivals that featured other sports as well. After the campaign of conquest by Alexander the Great (336–323 BC), who opened up the East to Greek cultural influences, hippodromes were built in the newly founded Hellenic cities, and chariot races were organized there on the

Greek model, with drivers competing on their own account rather than for factions. These events never matched the popularity of Roman chariot races.

Nevertheless, the ancient Greek variant had been in existence here for centuries. In the second century AD there was actually an upturn in public interest, probably inspired by the Hellenophile emperors Trajan and Hadrian, who encouraged chariot racing and had no objection to the sport being organized along Greek lines. New hippodromes were built in a range of towns in eastern regions of the Roman Empire. Major cities including Antioch, Caesarea, Antinoopolis, Gerasa, Bostra, Laodicea, and Tyre, important places within the structure of Roman provincial government, were endowed with arenas modeled on the great Circus Maximus.

The fourth century marked the breakthrough of the Roman variant in the East, and municipal governments gradually went over to the faction system, with permanent racing stables. Change came sooner in some cities than in others. As early as the final decades of the third century, Alexandria had full-fledged racing stables, whereas in Constantinople they did not become properly established until about 380.[1] The decision by the authorities in these cities to opt for the Roman variant was no doubt prompted by financial rather than merely sporting considerations. Wealthy families had always been willing to finance festivals voluntarily, to demonstrate their benevolence toward their cities, but they had not come through the economic crisis of the third century unscathed. They were forced to put on smaller shows, which were less attractive to the general public. The express involvement of the four racing stables in the organization of events meant the financial responsibility could be spread more broadly. By the early fifth century practically all the cities of the East had moved over to the faction system.

Radicalization in Rome

In fourth-century Rome chariot racing was still immensely popular, perhaps more popular than ever. The decline in that rival entertainment, the gladiator shows, was no doubt a major contributory factor.

Christian emperors could not permit themselves any real enthusiasm for a spectacle that in the past had cost many of their fellow believers their lives. They did not actually ban gladiator fights, but they did make clear to the organizers that they should not expect any official subsidy. In this they could count on the support of a majority of the population, which had converted to Christianity and no longer wanted to watch cruel shows in the Colosseum. The chariot races profited from the increasing aversion to gladiator fights, and emperors (or city prefects) shrewdly capitalized on this trend. To an even greater extent than before, emperors regarded the Circus Maximus as a vast meeting place where they could gauge the mood of the population and defend themselves directly in the face of their subjects' grievances.

Yet something does seem to have changed in this period in the attitude of the crowd. No matter how it behaved in the first two centuries of the imperial era, whether it controlled itself or let rip, whether disturbances broke out or not, the problems had always been manageable. In the mid-third century, as a result of the weakening of central authority, a turning point arrived, and the Senate and people of Rome increasingly set a course of their own. The emperors were patently finding it harder to keep the people in check. The fourth-century historian Ammianus Marcellinus, the last great heathen author in a world that was quickly converting to Christianity, wrote openly in his *Roman History* about the decline in discipline and the falling away of norms and values in Rome.[2] He plainly idealized a past in which Rome was governed by people who considered the traditional virtues to be of paramount importance. But that time was long gone. Now senators had mainly their own interests in mind; they had forgotten how Rome achieved greatness and held the whole world in its grasp. Now they rode through the city in luxurious coaches and wore ridiculously showy and expensive cloaks. The common folk were utterly degenerate, wine sodden; they spent their evenings and nights in wine houses, frittering away their time drinking and playing dice. During the day they visited theaters and circuses.

Ammianus blames the chariot races in particular. In the middle of his discourse on the degradation of Rome, he denounces the love of the populace for this particular spectacle, a love that verges on madness:

To them the Circus Maximus is a temple, a second home, a gathering place; in fact it is all their hope and desire. They hang around together on squares, at crossroads, in streets, and wherever they happen to meet. They have vehement quarrels with one another, and almost always one will argue for one racing stable, the other for another. Those among them who are already approaching the ends of their lives and have more authority on account of their advanced years swear by their wrinkles and their gray hair that the republic is finished if the driver they've put their money on doesn't shoot out of the starting stalls ahead of the rest in the upcoming chariot races but instead takes the turn too wide because his horses have been bewitched. However great their idleness and indifference, as soon as the longed-for day of the chariot races dawns, they dash as fast as their legs will carry them to the Circus, before sunrise, as if trying to outstrip the chariots that will compete in the races. Most are so nervous about all that they have to gain and to lose by the results that they can't relax the night before the races and don't sleep a wink.[3]

The passion among ordinary people for chariot racing was so extreme in this period that some charioteers acquired a more or less sacrosanct status and felt they could do whatever they liked—to the great annoyance of those in authority, who could only watch as people expressed support for these unruly performers. When in 355 the charioteer Philoromus was arrested on unspecified charges, the people saw it as sufficient reason to riot, and they attacked the city prefect Leontius. It took a vigorous response from him to restore order.[4]

In their efforts to put specific charioteers out of action, the authorities sometimes accused them of engaging in magic and sorcery. One of those so accused was a certain Hilarinus. In 364 city prefect Apronianus decided he was guilty of dark practices. He had sent his son to a sorcerer, asking him to impart to the boy the secrets of the black arts, so that in future he would have no need of strange magicians. Hilarinus was condemned to death and executed.[5] In 371 Auchenius and Athanasius met a similar fate, probably because Emperor Valentinianus had decided they were too popular and had too much influence with the people. His right-hand man, Maximinus, who led the purges, justified the arrest of the two charioteers by claiming they had practiced magic. He sentenced them to be burned to death. Whether the populace accepted the executions calmly or took to the streets to rob, loot, and commit arson is not mentioned by Ammianus, in whose work the anecdote about the deaths of the two men is to be found.[6]

For Christian authors it was an incontrovertible fact that the misconduct of charioteers and their supporters was a result of magic and witchcraft. A relatively unknown writer called Amphilochus of Iconium advances this view most clearly of all. In one of his poems he declares that contests on the racetrack were decided not by the speed of the four-horse chariots but by the dark arts, since in their insane longing for victories by their favorite stables the people turned to sorcerers and magicians, who duly invoked evil demons and with their aid made chariots collide or crash.[7] There was only one remedy: Christian prayer.

In writing about the common folk, Ammianus mentions something extraordinary, although only in a brief aside. Discussing the licentiousness of the populace, he mentions in passing the paid clappers in the Circus Maximus, meaning people hired to applaud for a fee or to orchestrate jeers of disapproval.[8] This is important because he is the first writer ever to mention the presence of "cheerleaders" at chariot races. They were already a familiar feature in Rome, since from the beginning of the imperial era they had been employed in the theater by actors, especially mime artists, who wanted to be certain of receiving enough applause. They discharged their task with such energy that they fairly regularly caused riots both inside and outside the theater and were banished from the city as a result, but until the fourth century they had not been used in the Circus Maximus.

For some scholars the absence of paid clappers is reason enough to assume that before their introduction in the Circus Maximus there were no riots of any significance and that spectators at chariot races, without rabble-rousers to provoke them, behaved with far more discipline than theater audiences. Whether you agree with this or not—as I have already indicated, I regard it as improbable that the crowds in the Circus Maximus were quiet and disciplined and suspect they frequently indulged in violence—there is no getting around the fact that in late antiquity the atmosphere at the racetrack underwent a significant change.

The use of paid clappers undoubtedly contributed to this. Whereas previously the anger had arisen and been discharged spontaneously, it was now deliberately worked up to a climax. Since this occurred with great regularity, the supporters' groups became more extreme—and more violent.

Nor were the factions any longer purely supporters' organizations, interested primarily in what happened on the track. They now played a far more active role in channeling the feelings of the crowd, which made itself heard in a more targeted manner than before. We have no way of knowing exactly how this change took place within the factions or at what point the use of paid clappers in the Circus Maximus became the norm. Nor is it clear whether the initiative came from actors, who perhaps approached the factions and offered to hire out their clappers for use in the circus, or from the leaders of the factions, who saw it as a way of gaining a better grip on their supporters. All we know for certain is that their appearance in the circuses led to an increase in political engagement on the part of the factions. Acting on behalf of the leaders of the factions, the clappers intimidated their own supporters. They forced them, so to speak, to amplify their applause, jeers, or curses. The emperor, or outside Rome the city prefect or provincial governor, found himself confronted with factions that knew better than before exactly how far they could go. Sometimes an organizer had no choice but to enter into consultation with the leaders of the factions to prevent trouble at the circus from escalating. An emperor or governor could not simply give the factions the freedom to behave in ways that were offensive from his own point of view. In late antiquity the emperor was more aware than anyone that in Rome (and to an even more worrisome degree in cities elsewhere in the Roman Empire) the power of central authority to maintain order was seriously deficient.

It was not just the part played by supporters in the stands that had changed; the stables had too. Until the mid-third century they had supplied the organizers with horses, chariots, and drivers. As we have seen, they were independent organizations, each operating under the leadership of a *dominus factionis*, a president and director, who was usually drawn from the knightly class. They were commercial enterprises that handled a great deal of money, and they had always preserved their independence and their own separate identities. Precisely because the business aspect was so important, successful charioteers had not been able to penetrate the ranks of top management.

In the course of the third century AD the first major change came about in the way the racing stables functioned. It was a cautious change but unmistakable. An inscription mentions a certain Polyphemus, who was "master and charioteer" (*dominus et agitator*) of the Reds in Rome.[9] He had been given the title *factionarius*, "leader of the racing stable," which was a quite different job than that of the old *dominus factionis*, who bore overall responsibility. The authority of the new *factionarius* was limited to the races. He was there to ensure that the drivers and horses in his stable were good enough to compete with those of the other stables. He could best be described as a sporting director. The financial and commercial side of the business now came under the jurisdiction of a higher body, which in Rome was directly controlled by the emperor and in the provinces by the governors.

The involvement of the emperor was no longer purely formal. He saw to it that the racing stables—in late antiquity this meant primarily the Greens and the Blues—took responsibility for the smooth running of races. In other words, the racing stables that had once offered their services to the organizers, supplying them with horses, chariots, and drivers, now had to bear ultimate responsibility, working in cooperation with the emperor's superintendents. In early fifth-century Constantinople an official called an *actionarius*, filling a post specially created for the purpose by the emperor, controlled the financial administration of the theater and the Hippodrome. Far from all emperors sat firmly in the saddle, however, and cooperation between the two did not always run smoothly, which led to all manner of problems.

Emperor and Public in Constantinople

The popularity of chariot racing in the fourth century AD was unaffected by these organizational changes. The races drew huge crowds, not just in Rome but all across the empire. The large cities of the East, Constantinople foremost among them, had hippodromes in which Roman-style chariot races were now held, adhering to the same fixed format everywhere: the Blue and Green racing stables acted as organizers; the Whites and Reds seem to have disappeared from the scene or to have been marginalized, although occasionally they might suddenly become active again. Up in the stands crowds of Greens and Blues cheered their favorite drivers, egged on by paid clappers. The rivalry between the two factions was fiercer than ever, partly as a result of increased vested interests, since emperors did not just express a preference for one of the two racing stables, they carried it through to its logical conclusion by appointing prominent people in their favored factions to high office.

Emperors involved themselves in all kinds of practical matters, right down to the seating arrangements in the stands. Emperor Theodosius II (408–50) was the first, as far as we can say with any confidence, to have changed the seating arrangements in the Hippodrome in Constantinople. He was a fervent follower of the Greens, and one of the ways he demonstrated this was by positioning his fellow fans where they could communicate with him. Previously the Greens had always sat to the emperor's right on the same side, the eastern side of the track. From now on they were to sit to his left and diagonally opposite, so that he could see them. Some Greens were even given seats directly opposite the emperor's loge, traditionally the place for soldiers from the garrison. The change disadvantaged the Blues, who now sat on the same side as the emperor, losing eye contact with him.[10]

This move by Theodosius II caused even greater rivalry between the Greens and the Blues. The Greens were proud that the emperor had set himself up as their patron and quite openly behaved as his clients. At the same time, knowing they were his favorites, they demanded that in return for their support he should continually do them favors. If he did not, or not to their satisfaction, they reacted immediately by running amok and creating disturbances out of sheer frustration, which the emperor then had to put down. After peace had been restored, he was confronted with a choice between continuing to support the Greens and siding with the Blues, for a short while at least. Like Theodosius, most emperors remained loyal to the Greens, but there were some who withdrew their support and openly sided with the Blues, thereby falling out with the Greens. Sometimes an emperor became muddled and did not know which of the two to back. Supporters would notice this immediately and make very clear that they had. If the emperor did not succeed in regaining the trust of at least one of the two main factions, he would very likely face mass protests. The Nika riot of 532 demonstrates where this could lead.

The attitude shown by Theodosius II marked the start of a powerful politicization of the factions, which played their new role with verve. It became the custom that the new emperor, as soon as he took office, would be presented to the people in the Hippodrome. Only after he had been greeted by the crowd of eighty thousand gathered there was he seen as officially having mounted the imperial throne.[11] In this ceremony an important role was reserved for the racing stables. One side, if not both, would cheer the new emperor. The supporters of a faction that did not show much enthusiasm, out of frustration at the knowledge that the emperor's sympathies lay with the other racing stable, faced difficult times ahead.

The decision by Theodosius II to give the Greens the best seats was not sufficient reason for them to follow him and his successors in everything. Even during the last few years of his reign the Greens caused minor riots, and several years after his death they had a public quarrel with his successor, Marcian (450–57). Perhaps they thought they could count on preferential treatment from him as well and resorted to violence when that turned out not to be the case. Marcian put down the riots and decided that in future no Green would be allowed to hold public office. Chrysaphius, one of the confidants of Theodosius II and a patron of the Greens, was beheaded. The official reason was that he had incited the Greens to violence. Now the emperor's preference lay with the Blues.

In the final decades of the fifth century the frequency of riots in Constantinople increased dramatically. To some extent they were a result of a hardening conflict between orthodox Christians and heretics. It is difficult to be sure whether the factions as organizations played any part in these quarrels, but most of the riots arose directly from the growing animosity between the Greens and the Blues. At first the response of the authorities was limited to arrests among the leaders of the factions. Sometimes this worked, but quite often the followers of whichever faction had been punished took to the streets and picked fights with supporters of the opposition. This often meant that before long large crowds were rampaging the streets, smashing and burning. It was fairly common for them to join forces and attack the police. This kind of uproar could usually be suppressed without bloodshed, but on several occasions it resulted in a large number of casualties.

In the late fifth century truly huge riots erupted. Constantinople was the setting for serious disturbances with particular regularity, but other hippodromes in the East were subject to severe disorder from time to time as well. The usual trigger for a riot was an argument between Greens and Blues that got out of hand. One disturbance in Antioch in 489, the penultimate year of the reign of Emperor Zeno, was particularly vicious. The violence was no less serious than it would be in Constantinople a couple of years later: the same street attacks, with murder, manslaughter, and arson, the same aggrieved attitude on one side or the other, in this case the Greens, and the same tough response by the authorities.

In 491, after the ascent to the throne of Emperor Anastasius, Constantinople was shaken by riots yet again. Many felt the emperor had been asking for trouble. Apart from the fact that he held deviant religious views (he was an adherent of Monophysitism),[12] in the first year of his reign he had shown himself to be averse to major chariot-racing shows. The frustrated supporters, both Greens and Blues, were furious. They cursed Anastasius and set fires all over the city, even burning down part of the Hippodrome.

Two years later there was a repeat performance when riots in the theater spread to the Hippodrome. The mob tore statues of the emperor and his wife from their pedestals and dragged them through the streets. Everywhere arson and vandalism erupted. Anastasius was pelted with stones and needed a police cordon. He had great difficulty subduing the parties to the conflict. Many of the ringleaders were arrested and executed.

After five years of relative peace, riots broke out again in 498, sparked by the Greens, who misbehaved in the streets and in the Hippodrome, throwing stones and setting fires. Several were arrested by the city prefect. On the next race day the fans asked Anastasius to release the prisoners, but the emperor ignored their request. A large group of supporters then gathered in front of the emperor's loge and threw stones at Anastasius. One almost hit him. The emperor's bodyguard pounced on the culprit and killed him, whereupon his friends became furious and set fires all over the place. Firm action by imperial troops was needed to restore order. Many Greens were killed. The situation returned to normal only after the emperor had undertaken to appoint a prominent Green as city prefect.

Constantinople remained restless throughout the early decades of the sixth century. There were several riots, large and small, some started by the Greens, others by the Blues. The immediate causes are by no means always clear, but most riots seem to have broken out simply because Anastasius, who was indecisive and far from popular, gave the factions every possible pretext for turning against him in the theaters and in the Hippodrome and could not come up with any response to their violent protests. In 501, during a major festival, disaster struck. The Greens suddenly attacked the Blues and killed several of their number, including the emperor's illegitimate son. Three years later there were again multiple fatalities in the Hippodrome, among them another of Anastasius's sons. In the years that followed, right up until Anastasius's death in 518, the Hippodrome repeatedly descended into turmoil.

These disturbances show that Greens and Blues could make life extremely difficult for an emperor. Worst of all, there was a risk that unrest would spread from Constantinople to provincial towns. Contact between members of the factions in different regions was so intense by this time that there was a real danger Greens or Blues from other places might come to the scene of the riots to lend their support or disturb the peace in their own hometowns. The sources repeatedly mention the close bonds of friendship between Greens in Antioch and Greens in Constantinople. An emperor who wanted to punish a faction in the capital would do well to be aware of the need to call to order factions of the same color elsewhere in the empire at the same time.

The historian Procopius wrote about of the behavior of the most fanatical supporters of the Greens and Blues and the fear they inspired in others.[13] Crowds sang their own warrior songs, with texts full of taunts aimed at hated opponents. Their peculiar haircut and clothing made them recognizable in the streets from far off. They grew their beard and moustache long in the style of the ancient Persians and cropped their hair close to the scalp in the front and at the temples, letting it grow down over their shoulders at the back. They went about wrapped in long, multicolored cloaks with gold stitching, concealing their daggers beneath them in daytime. When darkness fell they cast caution aside, pulled out their daggers, and strode through the city in gangs. These hooligans made the streets unsafe. They attacked passersby, committed terrible crimes of violence, and left a trail of destruction behind them. Most supporters were not as radical as this "hard core," but the emperors knew it would not take very much for the rabble-rousers to turn yet more of them into hooligans.

You might think, given that Greens and Blues were mainly out to cause widespread dislocation, that the emperors would have clamped down on the chariot races or at least challenged the authority of the factions. They could have cut back on the number of shows as a way of curbing the worst of the aggression. Anastasius must have considered doing this, but no doubt he dismissed the idea very quickly, since any such measure would inevitably have met with a hostile response. During his reign in particular, the chariot races were immensely popular, largely as a result of performances by top charioteers like Porphyrius, Julianus, Faustinus, and Constantinus, who, as we shall see, sent the crowd wild time and again. If Anastasius had taken it into his head to block this popular safety valve, he would surely have met with massive resistance.

He seems to have camouflaged his lack of love for chariot racing in a thoroughly novel way. He suddenly declared himself a follower of the Reds, a stable that had faded into the background along with the Whites amid the violence of the Greens and Blues, almost to the point of invisibility. This choice of a racing stable without many followers meant he could intervene in any conflict between Greens and Blues without being accused of bias. It also breathed new life into the Red faction, which saw a chance to play an important role again and even to attract top charioteers. Inadvertently, therefore, Anastasius's behavior led to an upturn in chariot racing.

CHAPTER 9

The Heroes of the Hippodrome

Enthusiasm for life as a charioteer was probably greater in Constantinople in the late fifth and early sixth centuries than it had ever been in Rome. Along with slaves and freedmen, citizens threw themselves into careers at the races. The main reason was that in the new capital a good driver had a far greater chance of improving his social position and gaining prestige in the world outside the arena than in Rome, where a charioteer remained a man of low status, his fame confined to the track. In Constantinople this had now changed, in the sense that an emperor might call upon a charioteer to assist him in difficult undertakings, especially military operations. A successful outcome meant a chance for him to grow into a true popular hero and raise his status even further.

Riots did not damage the popularity of the charioteers. As long as they continued to perform brilliantly on the racetrack, they were in effect unassailable. They flaunted their wealth, appeared in public ostentatiously dressed, and were proud of the fact that their heroic deeds would be commemorated by their fans with the erection of large gold, silver, and bronze public statues of them. A number of these stood on the *spina* at the Hippodrome, and so the heroes were always in the line of sight of their fans.

The place where the charioteers laid the foundations of their popularity, the Hippodrome, can tell us little about what went on there during a day of twenty-four races watched by a crowd eighty thousand strong. It is almost impossible to imagine what the Hippodrome looked like, either the arena or the stands, since hardly anything remains. All we are now able to determine is the shape of the racetrack, since it is still visible in the road around Sultanahmet Square, a road that describes precisely the angle of the turn in the ancient Hippodrome. The racetrack itself, like so many other structures of the Byzantine period, lies hidden under the streets and buildings of modern Istanbul. There are few traces of either the stands or the *spina*, partly because of looting by the Turks after they took Constantinople in 1453, although the Hippodrome had in fact been burned to the ground long before then in a major fire started by the Crusaders in 1204. A number of bronze statues, probably including those of famous charioteers that stood on top of the *spina*, were melted down. Only the four big bronze horses crowning the starting stalls were spared. The Crusaders took them back to Venice and set them above the entrance to St. Mark's. The Egyptian obelisk from around 1500 BC, known as the obelisk of Theodosius I, survived the period, although in a fractured state. It still stands "at the center of the racetrack," on a plinth decorated with reliefs on all four sides. They show Theodosius and his family accepting gifts from barbarians and presenting wreaths of honor to the winners of the races.

We have a number of descriptions by people who must have seen the Hippodrome at first hand, but they do little to help us form a precise impression. They are vague, with few technical details, and they offer no leads that might make a reasonably accurate reconstruction possible. The most informative is a fifteenth-century drawing by Onofrio Panvinio. He probably made his sketch shortly after the conquest of Constantinople in 1453. The Hippodrome is shown covered in sand, with a heavily built up urban district on one side and heaps of sand with houses between them on the other. To the right we can make out the starting stalls; in the middle of the racetrack stands the Egyptian obelisk placed there by Theodosius I, along with columns and plinths that probably once supported statues of charioteers. Nothing is left of the *spina* itself, although Robert of Clari, writing in 1204 shortly after the city was conquered by the Venetians, described it as a wall fifteen feet high and ten feet wide.

Porphyrius: An Exceptional Career

The years 500–540, during the reigns of Emperors Anastasius, Justin I, and Justinian, could confidently be called the highpoint of the history of chariot racing in Constantinople. A number of epigrams from this period have survived that make clear how much affection there was

Base of the obelisk on the *spina* in the Hippodrome in Constantinople, dating from AD 390. The reliefs on all four sides, one of which is shown here, reflect the imperial power of Theodosius I. (Photograph by Georges Jansoone)

among the general public for charioteers. Several of these epigrams were carved onto the plinths of statues erected in honor of specific drivers; others date from subsequent centuries. Even as late as the tenth century, Byzantine poets expressed their admiration for the top charioteers of those years.

The absolute star, popular with both the common folk and the emperors, was Porphyrius. We can reconstruct the general outlines of his career on the basis of thirty-two epigrams, some of which were carved on the bases of public statues.[1] These statues once stood on the *spina*, which in itself indicates that Porphyrius must have enjoyed extraordinary renown. The epigrams portray him as the favorite of the people of Constantinople, closely followed by his equally famous colleagues Julianus, Constantinus, Uranius, and Faustinus, who like him were immortalized in gold, silver, or bronze statues on the *spina*. Their mutual rivalry made the chariot races an exceptionally exciting spectacle.

Not much is known about Porphyrius as an individual; in fact, his childhood years are shrouded in the mists of time. The only firm fact is that he came from North Africa, from what is now Libya. We have no way of knowing how he ended up in Constantinople, whether he was discovered by scouts or came to the capital on his own initiative. The sources do not even have much to say about his later, extremely successful career. But by linking up the epigrams composed for him with a number of remarks by the sixth-century historian John Malalas it is possible to reconstruct the major events of his life.

The first specific mention of Porphyrius by Malalas tells us that in 507, under his second name, Calliopas, he was the leader (*factionarius*) of the Green stable. By then he had already made a name for himself in the racing world and was in a position few would achieve even by the late stages of their career. Perhaps even more striking is that he was a prominent political figure that year in Constantinople and that in the service of Emperor Anastasius he led the Greens in an attack on a synagogue in Daphne, a suburb of Antioch.[2] This indicates once again that successful charioteers were more than just heroes of the arena.

He must have made his way to the top very quickly indeed. At least, so one of the first epigrams about him, from around AD 500, implies. He was still a relatively unknown charioteer and not yet universally recognized as one of Constantinople's great talents. The text, a conversation between a stranger and Porphyrius, makes clear that Porphyrius must have begun chariot racing when he was very young.

Who are you, my dear young man? Your chin is only just covered
    in down.
Stranger, I am Porphyrius.
Where do you come from?
From Africa.
Who has honored you?
The emperor, for my races.
Who can testify to this?
The faction of the Blues.
Porphyrius, what you have earned is that Lysippus, a skillful
    sculptor, will commemorate your many victories.[3]

Despite his youth, Porphyrius had already made an impression. How old must he have been? Thirteen? Sixteen? Certainly no older. In the Circus Maximus, Crescens had been the youngest charioteer at thirteen years old,[4] while the great Diocles started relatively late, at eighteen.[5] The age of the average beginner must have been roughly sixteen.

There is another noteworthy aspect to this epigram. In his conversation with the unknown spectator, Porphyrius is a driver for the Blues, but as we have seen, seven years later, in 507, he was the leading man for the Greens. In the intervening years a great deal must have happened. His career probably went as follows: he became the leading driver for the Blues soon after 500 and was conspicuously honored for it with a bronze statue. Among the texts on its plinth was the following: "Victory gave you, Porphyrius, when you were still of a young age, this gift that time has given to others only reluctantly and late in their lives. Because, after she had added up all the performances that brought you many victory wreaths, she concluded that you stand far above the other drivers. What else is there for me to say? Did not even rival factions loudly applaud in admiration of your glory? Blessed is the very free people of the Blues, to whom the great emperor has entrusted you as a gift."[6]

Apparently this love was unrequited. The fans' eulogies were not enough for Porphyrius. No matter how fond the Blues were of him or how often they cheered him to victory, he was not dissuaded from taking a career path of his own, which led him to the Greens, probably because they were prepared to pay more for his services. No specific sums are mentioned, but they were undoubtedly substantial. With the Greens too he was a success, which yielded him another bronze statue, with various inscriptions. One of them reads: "Thrice chosen Porphyrius, the city desires to honor you with a bronze statue. It wishes the statue were of gold, but it had Nemesis in view. Still, if your patrons, members of the Green faction, never cease to celebrate your victories, to which they have grown accustomed, then all those people will be as many statues in your honor, and all gold is worthless compared to them."[7] Even the warm affection of the Greens, who had gone so far as to appoint him leader of their faction, was not sufficient to retain Porphyrius. A few years later he switched stables a second time. In

Rome he would probably have chosen the Whites or the Reds, but in Constantinople those factions were too small to meet his considerable demands, and so he once again performed on behalf of the Blues. That must have been after 507. His arrival was greeted by the fans of the Blues like the return of a prodigal son. Once more his qualities were elaborately praised: there is no better driver than Porphyrius, his skill with the reins is unequaled, he is the king of the racetrack.

Yet all this praise and the undoubtedly large sums of money the Blues paid out for him were not enough to bind Porphyrius to them for ever. He left again, and for the second time the Greens became his employers. His position as a famous charioteer was now apparently unassailable, since nobody even resented his changing sides this time. It seems rather as if he had outgrown the battle between factions to become public property. An inscription composed for him shortly after his move shows there was no animosity at all between the Greens and the Blues as a result of Porphyrius's transfer: "This Porphyrius was born in Africa, but brought up in Constantinople. He was regularly crowned with victory and he wore the highest symbols of conquest on his head, now driving for one, then for the other color. Often he changed faction and often he changed horses. Sometimes he was first, sometimes last, sometimes he finished in the middle group, and so he got the better of all his fans and all his opponents."[8]

Around the year 515 his popularity, even outside the racetrack and among those who were not particularly interested in chariot racing, must have grown considerably. For the second time he supported Emperor Anastasius at a difficult moment, on this occasion against a pretender to the throne called Vitalianus, who was of Gothic origin. Briefly it looked as though Vitalianus would seize power, but the revolt was put down, partly as a result of the actions of Porphyrius, who was assisting the emperor in his capacity as leader of the Greens, as the following epigram tells us: "Not only did divine Victory crown you during the races, in war too you emerged the winner, at the moment that the emperor, with the help of the Greens, fought a war against the wild frenzy of the enemy of the throne. When the savage tyrant died, just when Rome [meaning Constantinople] seemed to yield, the light of Latin freedom returned. For this reason the sovereign restored to the Greens the privileges they had previously enjoyed, and the artist made this beautiful polished statue."⁹ It was a highpoint in Porphyrius's career, but contrary to what we might expect in view of his immense success, the picture grows shadowy after this, and there are no texts that say anything about his achievements in the years that followed. It is impossible to tell how long Porphyrius remained active on the race-track and whether he switched stables again in those years. If he was roughly sixteen in 500, in 515 he was no older than thirty-one. He was probably in his prime at that point and went on to a string of further victories, but we hear nothing of them.

For a very long time, almost thirty years, the silence around Porphyrius is complete, and then suddenly there is a text in which he appears as an old but still successful charioteer: "When you were a young man, you defeated your elders; now that you are an old man yourself, you defeat the young men in *quadriga* races. Now that you have completed your six decades, Calliopas [the other name used by Porphyrius], you have earned a statue for your victories, by order of the emperor, so that your fame will be remembered by future generations. Oh, may your body be as immortal as your reputation."¹⁰

Porphyrius reached the age of sixty in about 544, during Justinian's reign. Precisely twelve years had now passed since the Nika riot, which led to a temporary ban on chariot racing. Only when Justinian was firmly in the saddle again did he dare to face the tumult of the chariot races, with fresh confrontations between the Greens and the Blues. Since few, if any, new drivers had been trained in the period the races had been suspended, the supporters turned to Porphyrius. At an advanced age he entered the arena again and won. The emperor and the people were unanimous in their tributes. It is one of the last ever testimonials to a great charioteer, one who had probably retired but returned to the arena at the request of his admirers and the organizers of the shows.

A sixty-year-old still active on the racetrack—it sounds a little strange to us, since we are used to thinking of sports figures as football players, athletes, and tennis players, whose careers are over by the age of about thirty-five, rather than jockeys. In the equestrian world, though, the age limit is far higher. Whether we look back to the charioteers of ancient Rome or to twentieth-century jockeys, in all eras there have been individuals who competed successfully at around the age of sixty against far young colleagues.

The most extraordinary example in Rome is Claudius Olympus. He was a less than top-ranking charioteer who had first appeared in the Circus Maximus under Nero (54–68). He built a solid reputation in the decades that followed and was still displaying his skills on the racetrack in 110, during the reign of Emperor Trajan. He must have competed for at least forty-two years.[11] He cannot have been the only man active for so long. No one tells us how many years Pompeius Musclosus, the driver with the greatest number of victories to his name, 3,559, took part in races, but if the proportion of starts made to victories achieved is the same as for Diocles, who won 1,462 times in a total of 4,257 races, a success rate of one in three, Musclosus must have lined up at the start well over 10,000 times. Even if he did much better than Diocles and finished half his races the winner, he must have made 7,000 starts, and if he took part in the same number of races per year as Diocles, 177, then he must have been active for at least forty years.

In the twentieth century several jockeys were famously active on the racetrack in their sixtieth year. The best known is the legendary Johnny Longden, an American jockey who died on 14 February 2003, on his ninety-sixth birthday. He achieved his first victory in 1927, his last on 12 March 1966. In December of that year, when he was almost sixty, he rode the last of a total of 32,413 races, of which he won 6,032, an unprecedented number. Longden's record has since been broken. The current holder is Laffit Pincay Jr., who began his career two years after Longden left the racetrack and had more than 9,500 victories to his name by the time he retired in 2003 at the age of fifty-six.[12]

With this in mind the length of Porphyrius's career is less astonishing than it appears at first sight. If we look at his competitors, it seems almost as if after the Nika riot the veterans ruled the roost. His greatest rivals were all of his own generation, with comparable careers behind them. Julianus, Constantinus, Uranius, and Faustinus were absolute winners like Porphyrius, and after careers with both the Greens and the Blues they too were blessed with victories in "old age." They were clearly overshadowed by Porphyrius, since fewer panegyrics about them have survived, but based on the written evidence we do have they must have been true greats as well. It could hardly be otherwise, since if Porphyrius had stood on a lonely pinnacle, without any real rivals, he would not have been such a celebrated competitor.

There was one event in which Porphyrius's superiority could not be relied upon and that was the *diversium*, which had once been performed in the Circus Maximus as well (see chapter 5). In Constantinople the *diversium* developed into a serious test of strength, more a battle between racing stables than a contest between individual drivers. The basic idea was the same as in Rome. Two races were combined in one event: in the first the drivers used their own chariots and their own horses; in the second they raced in chariots belonging to their opponents. There were two versions, differentiated by the role of the *hortatores*, the helpers, who in one case went over to the opponents' chariots along with their drivers and in the other remained with their own chariots and horses and helped the drivers from the other stable. The charioteer who won with his own helpers in a chariot belonging to the "enemy" received the prize money. If he achieved victory in an unfamiliar chariot with unfamiliar helpers, the prize money went to the other stable.

Constantinus must have mastered this event better than anyone. He was said to have driven in fifty races of this type in one day. He won the twenty-five races in his own *quadriga* effortlessly, and of the twenty-five in which he used chariots belonging to the opposition he won twenty-one.[13] Whether he defeated even Porphyrius in this event the epigram in the *Anthologia Palatina* does not tell us. Quite possibly the number of victories attributed to Constantinus is an exaggeration. Perhaps it is merely a product of the imagination of the panegyrist. Porphyrius himself was very proud that in a single day he had been victorious in two *diversium* races.

The lists of victories by Porphyrius, Constantinus, and the other charioteers whose achievements were set down in epigrams leave no room for doubt that the emperor and the public understood very clearly that theirs was a unique generation. It seems entirely natural that these heroes' likenesses were mounted above the emperor's loge as a tribute to their extraordinary feats.

CHAPTER 10

The Disappearance of Chariot Racing

Although in Constantinople the chariot races flourished around 500, the spectacle was suffering a serious decline in Rome. The political disintegration and economic malaise of the fifth century had finally taken their toll. Rome had seen its population fall at a great rate, with only 100,000 inhabitants left by 500. The Circus Maximus was rarely filled to capacity. The number of days reserved for chariot races had been reduced dramatically and the number of races per day cut to eight. Aside from money there was a shortage of good drivers. Even in the lowest strata of Roman society, at one time the breeding ground of charioteers, enthusiasm for a career on the racetrack was far less than it had once been. The *Codex Theodosianus* states in effect that to compensate for the lack of aspiring charioteers, people chosen more or less at random were being forced to report to the racing stables.[1] One direct consequence of the shortage of top-notch charioteers (and probably of top-notch horses as well) was that the training sessions had to be adjusted. The drivers were less appealing, which had repercussions for the popularity of the sport. The spectators stayed away, and the willingness to organize spectacular shows fell precipitately. Substantial prizes were still being put up, and the very best drivers could still become rich, but their wealth bore no comparison to that of the charioteers of the first two centuries AD. Moreover, the winner could by no means always be certain that he would receive his prize in cash, as there was a growing tendency to pay out prizes in kind, in the form of expensive clothes or precious stones.

For the average charioteer who had won few, if any, prizes, the struggle to survive became increasingly hard. Those who were still slaves could forget about ever being able to buy their freedom. Those granted liberty because their owners could no longer see any advantage in being responsible for them, given the poor economic climate, lived in permanent fear of being removed from their racing stables. Several were in fact reduced to beggary.

The then ruler of Italy, the Ostrogoth Theoderik (492–526), tried to breath new life into the chariot races, not because he was a great fan himself but because he respected old Roman traditions and recognized thrilling chariot races as a good means of securing the support of the people of the city. To attract sufficient charioteers he introduced a fixed basic salary, although it was no more than a paltry two solidi, a small sum compared with the earnings of even mediocre drivers in the glory days of the sport. Nor did it really help. The downward spiral continued. In the course of the sixth century chariot races slowly disappeared from the scene.

Cassiodorus, secretary to Theoderik until he withdrew from public life and founded a monastery in southern Italy, did not mourn the sport's passing. He felt chariot races undermined all feeling for moral values and were an invitation to childish behavior. They made people dismissive of virtue and decency, with disturbances and riots as an inevitable consequence.[2] When Cassiodorus wrote this, in the early 550s, he was worried that chariot racing would eventually be restored to its former glory, but in fact it already belonged to the past. The revival under the Ostrogoth Totila, who had organized chariot races in 549 to give an extra sparkle to the Byzantine celebrations of his conquest of Rome, would not recur.[3] This is the last ever mention in the sources of chariot races in Rome.

In stark contrast to the gradual disappearance of chariot racing from Rome are the massive shows put on in Constantinople, where chariot racing thrived in the years 500 to 550, featuring top charioteers of a caliber rarely seen before. But after the mid-sixth century, silence falls over Byzantine chariot racing as well. It still took place, the Hippodrome was still filled to capacity on regular occasions, and there were still riots, but something had changed. It is not at all easy to find an explanation for this drying up of information. It could be that the great personalities among the charioteers had gone, that the younger drivers who took over from them did not have as much charisma as their great predecessors and were therefore less appreciated by the public. But that would have applied only in the short term, for one or two generations at the most, not for the six centuries across which the races continued to be held. One contributory factor was undoubtedly the recurrent shortage of financial resources. Chariot racing was expensive, and the subsidies from the imperial treasury that had for so many years been handed out to the Greens and Blues to cover the costs of organizing races were now often unavailable or inadequate.

Emperor Tiberius II was the first to put a squeeze on resources. In 578 he reduced the imperial contribution to the factions because he believed they were spending money too freely. Perhaps he was sick of the violent behavior of hooligans among the Greens and the Blues. Sixteen years earlier, in 562, when Justinian was still emperor, fans had shown they had learned little from the Nika riot thirty years before. The worst of the troublemakers had caused destruction all over the city after leaving the Hippodrome. For a short time it had even looked as if another mass revolt would break out, but Justinian managed to restore order reasonably promptly on that occasion. In the years since then the threat of fresh disturbances had never completely lifted.

A number of subsequent emperors treated the circus factions much as Tiberius had done. In times of crisis especially, when all available financial resources were needed to pay for wars against the Arabs or other great powers, they cut contributions from the imperial treasury, so that the budgets of the Greens and the Blues dropped significantly and the shows became smaller in scope and therefore less attractive to the general public. Putting twenty-four races on a day's program, as had been the custom in the fifth and sixth centuries, was no longer feasible. By the tenth century the number had declined to eight.

What remained was the ceremonial focused on the emperor. A newly appointed emperor still went to the Hippodrome to be greeted by a large crowd, but the relationship between this ceremony and the chariot races was now less obvious. In Rome the fans had gone to the Circus Maximus for the chariot races, and contact with the emperor had been one feature of that experience. In Constantinople the significance of the ceremonial around the emperor greatly increased from the fifth century onward, although the chariot races remained crucial. No matter how popular the emperor was, without the racing he would have had considerable difficulty filling the Hippodrome.

Tiberius II changed the relationship between imperial ceremonial and charioteering. Contact between emperor and people was now the highpoint of a full day's program in the Hippodrome; the races were reduced to a mere accompaniment to the ceremonies. Understandably, the real fans were less than thrilled by this. For lack of sufficient evidence we cannot be certain of the extent to which later emperors stuck to the hard political line adopted by Tiberius II. All we know is that the few available sources speak of more sober, stripped-down shows for which the public exhibited little enthusiasm. The Greens and the Blues still sat in the Hippodrome and made their voices heard as they always had, but more as a reaction to an emperor's behavior (or misbehavior) than out of admiration for a dazzling racing event. Emperor Phocas, for example, was loudly abused by the Greens in 609 when he got very drunk as he sat watching the races, losing all sense of reality. He felt insulted by the hostile crowd and sent out a punitive expedition that cost many supporters their lives.

Confrontations of this kind occurred with greater regularity as time went on. Riots arising directly from the rivalry between Greens and Blues on the track are hardly ever mentioned in this later period. We hear even less about exciting races. Long before Constantinople was conquered by the Crusaders in 1204, the chariot races had in fact been reduced to a bare minimum, to a spectacle that had only its rich history to boast about and no longer an irresistible program of events.

CHAPTER 11

Ben-Hur

Chariot Racing
in the Movies

Chariot races and *Ben-Hur*. For many people the two are inseparable. The chariot race on the silver screen is so fascinating that it is still talked about half a century after the movie came out. *Ben-Hur* has been shown repeatedly on television and released on video and DVD, and so more and more people have seen the chariot racing sequence. Its astonishing fame made me eager to try to find out what the filmmakers had in mind when they decided to make such a feature of the race.

The movie is based on a novel of the same name by Lew Wallace, a lawyer and former army general from Indiana who had seen distinguished service in the Civil War. The story is long, deeply sentimental in parts, set during the life of Jesus against a background of ancient Judaism and an all-powerful Rome. The main theme is the battle between good and evil. Judah Ben-Hur, a Jew, is the personification of virtue, while Messala, a Roman, represents evil. Ben-Hur and Messala are childhood friends, but they grow apart until there could be no greater contrast between them. Ben-Hur is dedicated to the Jewish cause, while Messala sides unconditionally with Roman imperialism. Their relationship reaches a critical juncture after one particular incident. Messala accuses Ben-Hur of subversive activities and sends him to the galleys of the Roman fleet. Ben-Hur travels across barren terrain to Syria, and during the journey he meets a man he later learns to be Jesus, who gives him water. For three years he is forced to row in the fleet. During a sea battle he saves the life of the Roman consul Quintus Arrius, who responds by taking him to Rome and adopting him as his son. But Ben-Hur wants to return to Judea, to his mother, sister, and fiancée. In Jerusalem he finds only the last. Furious, he goes to see Messala, reporting to him as the son of Arrius. Their rivalry is reignited.

Then comes the chariot race in which they compete against each other. Ben-Hur wins; Messala is killed. Ben-Hur goes in search of his mother and sister and finds them in the valley of the lepers. At the same time, Jesus is being crucified. Ben-Hur recognizes him as the man who once gave him water. The story ends with Ben-Hur and his family happily reunited, forming part of the first Christian community.

When *Ben-Hur* was published in 1880, few people expected the book to sell particularly well, but after six months it suddenly made its breakthrough and went on to an unprecedented triumph. *Ben-Hur* conquered the United States, and Wallace became a famous author. A little more than a year after the book came out, he was sent to Turkey by President Garfield, supposedly to serve his country as U.S. special envoy, in reality to see with his own eyes the places in the Mediterranean world that he had described in his book without ever visiting them. In 1899 Wallace was granted the satisfaction of watching a play based on *Ben-Hur* on Broadway. The stage production was a great success and ran until 1920. It even included the chariot race, performed in a kind of treadmill. As the elderly Wallace watched the actors interpret his work, he is said to have exclaimed: "My God, did I set all of this in motion?"[1]

In Wallace's novel the showdown on the racetrack in Jerusalem between Ben-Hur and Messala is one of a series of climaxes. In all three *Ben-Hur* movies, released in 1907, 1925, and 1959, the chariot race is the single absolute climax. Even in the earliest version, barely twenty minutes long, director Sidney Olcott managed to film a real chariot race. There was no proper racetrack surrounded by tiers of seating— only twenty spectators were present—and the jerky frames show only a few minutes of racing, but Olcott set the tone for spectacular action sequences in movies.

By 1925, when *Ben-Hur* was filmed for the second time, again with an emphasis on the chariot race, Hollywood had gained considerable experience with showpiece scenes, and the crew took full advantage of existing know-how under the direction of Fred Niblo. A real racetrack was built. Forty-two cameramen shot hundreds of meters of film from different angles, and stuntmen were employed to make the racing as lifelike as possible. This *Ben-Hur* drew large audiences over a considerable period, in Europe as well as the United States, much to the annoyance of Mussolini, who could not bear to see Messala defeated by Ben-Hur. He banned the movie in Italy. Surely no Jew could be superior to a Roman.

In 1959 the third version of *Ben-Hur* opened, directed by William Wyler. When he was offered the job, he is said to have responded that he only wanted to film the chariot race. In the end he agreed to take on the whole film, but it is clear from the chariot race and the sea battle in which Ben-Hur saves the life of consul Quintus Arrius that the spectacular sequences were the parts on which the director focused most of his attention. His depiction of the race made such an impact that *Ben-Hur* and chariot racing have been inseparable in the public mind ever since.

The budget Wyler had at his disposal, fifteen million dollars, an astronomical sum in those days, enabled him to design a proper Roman circus, complete with a richly decorated *spina*, real chariots, and actors (or stuntmen) who spent a full three months performing daredevil feats in front of the cameras. The result is truly impressive, a chariot race lasting almost nine minutes, roughly the time the charioteers in the Circus Maximus took to cover their seven laps, complete with cheating and crashes. After half a century, the chariot race has lost none of its power.

Ben-Hur (Charlton Heston) and Messala (Stephen Boyd) drive up to the starting line along with seven other charioteers. They are a mixed bunch, from all over the empire: Alexandria, Messina, Carthage, Cyprus, Rome, Corinth, Athens, Phrygia, and Judea. At the start the horses wait restlessly. Then they are off. Messala immediately pulls into the lead. One of the chariots takes the turn too tightly and crashes. Then the camera focuses on Messala. On the second lap he swerves out wide in his special chariot, which has jagged blades sticking out of the axles. They gouge deep into the Cypriot's wheels. The wreckage of the smashed chariot has barely been cleared away when Messala claims his next victim. This time it is the turn of the Corinthian. The driver is thrown out of his chariot and dragged along the track. He manages to free himself and avoid the hooves of the team behind him as it storms his way, but not the team that comes after it. The helpers who rush to his aid scoop him up and hurriedly carry him off the track. They are back in action immediately, since Messala has again forced a rival chariot out of the race, the Phrygian this time, who in his efforts to avoid the blades has driven too close to the *spina* and crashed.

Up to this point Ben-Hur has remained in the background. We see him occasionally, in close-up, looking strained. But when the Athenian and Carthaginian charioteers crash and Ben-Hur cannot avoid the smashed wreckage, he becomes the central figure. His chariot is tossed into the air by the debris, dislodging him. It takes him a huge effort to climb back on board. In the sixth lap the real battle between Messala and Ben-Hur begins. Ben-Hur has moved ahead and now threatens Messala's lead. Messala does all he can to force his enemy off the track. He attempts to twist his blades into the wheels of Ben-Hur's chariot, but Ben-Hur evades him with a series of deft maneuvers, although some of the superstructure of his chariot is chewed away.

Then comes the climax. Provoked to a frenzy, Messala lashes Ben-Hur with his whip, which Ben-Hur manages to grab. Ferocious pushing and pulling follows. Nevertheless, Messala seems to have won when his blades come dangerously close to the wheel of Ben-Hur's chariot and threaten to chop through it. But they do not. They impact the hard wood of the axle and are stuck. Messala's chariot is lifted into the air, flinging him out. The contest is over. Messala is dragged along by his four horses. He does manage to free himself from the reins, but in the end he is trampled by the *quadriga* from Alexandria. The final frames of the race show the victorious Ben-Hur, who, after crossing the finishing line, drives past the shattered body of the mortally wounded Messala.

The chariot race is magnificently filmed, and in parts it could be described as bloodcurdling. But is it a faithful reconstruction? Were the filmmakers sincerely trying to portray Roman charioteering as accurately as possible? Or did they realize there were a good few differences between Greek and Roman chariot races and, since they had been asked to locate their race in Jerusalem, in the eastern part of the Roman Empire,[2] decide to let their imaginations rip? The solution they came up with was spectacular, and it lies somewhere between the two forms of chariot racing. Elements from both types of event, the Greek and the Roman, have been adopted without anyone paying much attention to how hard they might be to reconcile.

The stadium in which the race is held is typically Roman. The tiers of seating, the racetrack, the *spina*—all are reminiscent of a Roman circus. Least realistic is the starting line, which lacks the high stalls out of which the chariots of antiquity poured as the race began. The track itself, however, looks extremely authentic. Like the Romans of two thousand years ago, the designers of the film set needed somehow to create an arena in which the horses could reach maximum speed without being hidden from spectators by the dust they churned up. At first they tried pouring a layer of fine lava chippings twenty-five centimeters thick on top of a layer of compacted, finely ground stone. Twenty centimeters of yellow sand was then dumped on top. But after just one day of rehearsals it was clear that the horses were sinking deep into the sand and could not get up enough speed. Everything was removed, apart from four centimeters of the lava chippings, which proved thick enough to give the horses sufficiently soft ground.[3] No solution was found to the billowing up of fine dirt. The track was sprinkled with water regularly but moderately, since if it was too wet the horses would be slowed down. The drivers all had to wear specially designed contact lenses to protect them from grit and loose stone chippings, which raises an unanswerable question: How did the charioteers of ancient Rome cope with those clouds of dust?

The chariots used in the film are neither Roman nor Greek. The racing chariots of antiquity were very light, no more than thirty-five kilograms, whereas those in *Ben-Hur* weighed well over two hundred. According to Marcus Junkelmann, the wrong prototype was chosen.[4] The Romans had two kinds of chariots: the true racing chariot, and the victory chariot, which was heavier and more cumbrous (see chapter 4). The filmmakers, for reasons that remain unclear, chose the second type and then made the chariots even heavier by constructing them out of steel tubing and thick planks instead of thin wooden slats and flexible basketwork, so the horses could race at top speed only for a short time, no more than one or two laps, nothing like the seven laps that were run at a fantastic pace on the Roman tracks. One reason for making the chariots heavier may have been a concern for the safety of the actors and stuntmen. In antiquity many charioteers were killed on the racetrack. Standing in their small, lightweight chariots, they were at continual risk of being flung out. The producers could not afford accidents like that and therefore opted for heavier chariots. The decision was made easier by the size of the horses. Seventy-eight thoroughbreds were selected in what was then Yugoslavia, large animals, much taller than any horse ever seen in the Circus Maximus (see chapter 4). They could be hitched to larger vehicles, and as long as certain film techniques were used, it would still seem as if the charioteers were standing in tiny chariots. Ben-Hur's white horses in particular, thoroughbred Lippizaners, look extremely impressive.

Although the circus appears to be Roman, the race unfolds before the crowd in the Greek style. The charioteers look Greek, with colorful robes that betray an Eastern influence. Ben-Hur alone is wearing a Roman outfit, with strapping as armor, a dagger, and a leather helmet, which, notably, he removes just before the race. All nine charioteers drive in the style of participants in the Olympic Games and other chariot races in ancient Greece, with the reins in both hands rather than wound around their body in the Roman manner.

Perhaps most telling of all is that the nine drivers, who come from all points of the compass, compete for individual honor rather than as members of one of the racing stables that called the shots in Rome. This is logical, since in the first century AD the racing stable system with its supporters' factions had not yet been fully introduced in the eastern half of the Roman Empire. It has to be said that the individualist style of competition adds to the excitement. There is no collaboration. Each man competes on his own account, and ultimately Ben-Hur is the supreme winner.

We are told nothing about the social background of Ben-Hur's rivals. It is clear that not all of them have been drawn from the ranks of slaves and freedmen. Ben-Hur, the adopted son of the Roman consul Quintus Arrius, actually belongs to the aristocratic elite. In Olympia he would not have been out of place among the participants, but in Rome he would have stepped into the arena only in the period before his adoption became final, when he was Quintus Arrius's slave. Perhaps Quintus Arrius is alluding to this during the feast at which he announces that he has adopted Ben-Hur, when he says that his new son has driven his horses to victory five times.

During the race much happens that could not have occurred during either a Greek or a Roman chariot race but which is entirely a product of the imagination of Lew Wallace and the scriptwriters. We have seen that all kinds of behavior were allowed in the ancient arenas. Lashing at other horses with the whip and swinging out wide to push an opponent off the track were regarded as permissible tactics. But what Messala resorts to in his determination to win would not have been tolerated on any racetrack. Fitting his chariot with blades that stuck out of the axles, purely in order to eliminate his opponents, would have been enough to get him removed from the track immediately by the head umpire. Even if he had got through the pre-race checks, it is inconceivable that the crowd would have accepted his participation in the race. It is easy to imagine what would have happened had he appeared at the starting line. The crowd would have jeered and chanted, demanding he be removed from the racetrack. The spectators might even have stormed the track and lynched the cheating charioteer. It is even conceivable they would have turned against the organizing committee, with the attendant risk of an outbreak of widespread rioting.

In the movie none of this matters, and the spectators are enthralled no matter whether anyone cheats or not. The chariot with the rotating blades suits the evil Messala perfectly. That is the difference between reality and fiction, between the real charioteers of the ancient world and the dreamed-up heroes of the silver screen.

LIST OF RACETRACKS

I have written mainly about races in the Circus Maximus in Rome and the Hippodrome in Constantinople. Scattered all across the Roman Empire were many other racetracks, at least a hundred of them. Here is a list of the most important tracks of which the interior dimensions are known. Fractions of meters have been rounded off. The figures are based on those given in Humphrey 1986.

Alexandria (Egypt), 450 by 52 m
Antinoopolis (Egypt), 440 by 58 m
Antioch (Syria), 492 by 70–75 m
Aquileia (Italy), 450 by 76 m
Arles (France), 400–450 by 84 m
Bostra (southern Syria),
    420 by 83–97 m
Bovillae (Italy, not far from Rome),
    350 by 60 m
Caesarea Maritima (Israel),
    450 by 90 m
Carthage (Tunisia), 500 by 78 m
Constantinople (Turkey),
    400 by ? m
Cyrene (Libya), 351 by 58 m
Dougga (Tunisia), 300 by ? m
Gerasa (Jordan), 244 by 51 m
Gortyn (Crete), 400 by 68 m
Leptis Magna (Libya), 450 by 70 m

Merida (Spain), 404 by 96 m
Milan (Italy), 460 by 67–68 m
Rome, Circus Maxentius,
    503 by 75–79 m
Rome, Circus Maximus,
    550–580 by 80 m
Rome, Circus Varianus,
    565 by 115–125 m
Rome, Circus Vaticanus,
    560 by 80 m
Saguntum (Spain), 354 by 73 m
Sirmium (Serbia), 430 by 70 m
Thessaloniki (Greece), 400 by 73 m
Thysdrus (Tunisia), 470 by ? m
Toledo (Spain), 408 by 86 m
Trier (Germany), 440 by 80 m
Tyre (Lebanon), 450 by 86 m
Vienne (France), 441 by 101 m

NOTES

Introduction

1. In *Satires* 10.77–81, Juvenal wrote: "For a long time already, since no one pays for their votes, the people have abdicated their duties; the public that once bestowed military commands, consulships, legions—everything, now keeps quiet and longs for just two things: bread and circuses." [Most passages from ancient texts have been translated by me from the Dutch. In the few instances in which existing English translations have been used, they are credited in the endnotes.—Trans.] Juvenal is also referring to gladiatorial combat in the Colosseum, but his conscious choice of the word *circenses* suggests that the *ludi circenses* (in other words, chariot races) were even more popular than the gladiator shows.

2. There are several excellent studies, among them Cameron 1973 and 1976, Humphrey 1986, Junkelmann 1990, and Horsmann 1998.

Chapter 1: The Nika Riot

1. All were regarded as heretics. It was said that for a long time the Samaritans had not been monotheists but worshiped many gods. Later they switched to a single god, the god of the Jews, but a rift developed between them and the Jews, at which point they founded a temple of their own, where they worshiped their own god.

Manichaeans believed there was a primal conflict between light and dark, between good and evil. Believers set themselves the aim of liberating light particles that belonged to the world of light, which the demons had devoured and encased in matter.

2. Procopius, *History of the Wars* 1, 24.54; John Malalas, *Chronographia* 18, 71 (p. 476), speaks of thirty-five thousand victims.

Chapter 2: Chariot Races of the First Century BC and Earlier

1. Homer, *Iliad* 23, 262–652.
2. Pausanias, *Description of Greece* 6, 20.10–19.
3. Ibid. 6, 19.10–21.1.
4. Humphrey 1986, 7.
5. Sophocles, *Electra* 671–753.
6. Pliny the Elder, *The Natural History* 8, 65.161–62.
7. Livy, *History of Rome* 1, 9.
8. Ibid. 1, 35.7–9.
9. Ibid. 1, 35.9.
10. This matter is dealt with in detail by Bernstein 1998, 313–50.

Chapter 3: The Circus Maximus

1. Livy, *History of Rome* 2, 31.3.
2. Ibid. 8, 20.
3. Suetonius, *Lives of the Twelve Caesars: Julius Caesar*, 39.2–3; Dionysius of Halicarnassus, *Roman Antiquities* 3, 68.1–4.
4. Suetonius, *Lives of the Twelve Caesars: Claudius*, 21.3.
5. *Corpus Inscriptionum Latinarum* 6, 944. English translation taken from *The Gospel of Matthew in Its Roman Imperial Context*, by John Kenneth Riches and David C. Sim (London, 2005).
6. Pliny the Younger, *Panegyricus Traiani*, 51.2–5.
7. Scriptores Historiae Augustae, *Antoninus Pius*, 9.1; *Chronica Minora* 146.
8. *Chronica Minora* 147.
9. Ibid. 148.
10. Dionysius of Halicarnassus, *Roman Antiquities* 3, 68.1–4.
11. Pliny the Elder, *The Natural History* 36, 24.103.
12. Humphrey 1986, 126.
13. Ovid, *The Art of Love* 1, 135–62.
14. See Humphrey 1986, 157–70, and Junkelmann 1990, 111.
15. Cassiodorus, *Variae epistulae* 3, 51; see also Tertullian, *De spectaculis* 8.
16. For an extensive, very thorough treatment of all the separate elements of the *spina*, see Humphrey 1986, 255–94.
17. Cassius Dio, *Roman History* 55, 10.8.

Chapter 4: Preparation and Organization

1. The observation by Tertullian, *De spectaculis*, 9.5, that the Reds and the Whites existed even back in the time of the kings and that the Blues and the Greens emerged only at the start of the imperial era has been dismissed convincingly by Cameron 1976, 56–61.

2. Tertullian, *De spectaculis*, 9.5; Isidore of Seville, *Origenes* 18, 41.

3. Cassius Dio, *Roman History* 61, 6.3.

4. The most extensive description is *Inscriptiones Latinae Selectae* 5313.

5. I have adopted this suggestion from Junkelmann 1990, 152.

6. Ibid., 38–53.

7. *Corpus Inscriptionum Latinarum* 6, 37834; see also Horsmann 1998, 294–96.

8. See Hyland 1990, 209.

9. Galenus, *De methodo medendi* 10, 478.

10. Martial, *Epigrams* 10, 9.

11. Saint John Chrysostom, *Homilies* 48.

12. This description is based on Junkelmann 1990, 144–45, and Junkelmann in Köhne, Ewigleben, and Jackson 2000, 91–92.

Chapter 5: A Day at the Circus Maximus

1. Juvenal, *Satires* 9, 142–44.

2. Suetonius, *Lives of the Twelve Caesars: Caligula*, 26.

3. Scriptores Historiae Augustae, *Heliogabalus*, 23.1–2.

4. Juvenal, *Satires* 3, 60–68; Cyprian, *De spectaculis* 5.

5. The opening procession is described by Dionysius of Halicarnassus, *Roman Antiquities* 7, 72.

6. Satyrs and sileni were types of woodland spirits. They were imagined as half human, half animal, with hooves, horns, tails, and large phalluses. They personified the uncontrolled sensual instincts.

7. Ovid, *The Loves* 3, 2.65–84; English translation by Guy Lee in *Ovid's Amores* (London, 1968).

8. Sidonius Apollinaris, *Carmina* 23, 307–427. The "field of Elis": he is referring to the Olympic Games. "Your partner does likewise": the four chariots were apparently paired up. The charioteers tried either to win themselves or to ensure that the drivers they were paired with would win.

9. Cassius Dio, *Roman History* 59, 7.2.

10. Ibid. 60, 27.2.

11. Suetonius, *Lives of the Twelve Caesars: Domitian*, 4.3.

12. Here I take my lead from Horsmann 1998, 93–94 n. 8.

13. Suetonius, *Lives of the Twelve Caesars: Augustus*, 43.

14. See Hyland 1990, 221.

15. Cassiodorus, *Variae Epistulae*, 3.51.9.

16. Pliny the Elder, *The Natural History* 8.65.160.

17. *Corpus Inscriptionum Latinarum* 6, 10048; Martial, *Epigrams* 10, 53.

18. Martial, *Epigrams* 10, 53.

19. *Corpus Inscriptionum Latinarum* 6, 10078.

20. Pliny the Elder, *The Natural History* 28.72.237.

21. Silius Italicus, *Punica* 16, 303–456.

Chapter 6: The Heroes of the Arena

1. Horsmann 1998, 172–306.

2. I base this on ibid., 73–77; Horsmann gives a good analysis of the *Tabula Larinas,* on which the relevant text is found. It states that the ban also applied to freeborn women (*ingenuae*) aged under twenty, but I think that in their case only playacting was meant.

3. *Corpus Inscriptionum Latinarum* 6, 10050.

4. Ibid., 10062.

5. Ibid., 10049.

6. *Inscriptiones Latinae Selectae* 5283.

7. *Corpus Inscriptionum Latinarum* 2, 4314.

8. The inscription is analyzed in detail by F. Drexel in Friedländer 1921, 179–85.

9. These figures are to be found in Duncan-Jones 1982.

10. Juvenal, *Satires* 7, 112–114; I have taken both examples from Horsmann 1998, 147–48.

11. Martial, *Epigrams* 10, 74.1–6, and 10, 76.8.

12. Ibid. 4, 67.5–8.

13. Ibid. 10, 50.

Chapter 7: The Spectators

1. Here I take the low number of 150,000 from Dionysius of Halicarnassus, *Roman Antiquities* 3, 68.3. Pliny the Elder, *The Natural History* 36, 102, writes of a capacity of 250,000.

2. Martial, *Epigrams* 8, 11.

3. Cassius Dio, *Roman History* 73, 13.3–4.

4. Flavius Josephus, *Jewish Antiquities* 19, 24–27. Cassius Chaerea was

a lieutenant of the Praetorian Guard, who despite his martial bearing was continually ridiculed by Caligula on account of his high-pitched voice.

5. *Inscriptiones Latinae Selectae*, 8753; Audollent 1904, no. 286. English translation taken from Hyland 1990, 229–30.

6. *Corpus Inscriptionum Latinarum* 8, 12508; Audollent 1904, no. 237.

7. Audollent 1904, no. 187.

8. Pliny the Elder, *The Natural History* 7, 186.

9. Pliny the Younger, *Letters* 9, 6.

10. Augustine, *Sermo de dilectione dei et proximi* 9.

11. Tacitus, *Dialogue on Oratory* 29.

12. Tacitus, *The Annals* 14, 14.1.

13. Ibid. 15, 67.2.

14. Pliny the Younger, *Letters* 9, 23.

15. The texts that bring out the attitude to the Circus Maximus among the elite can be found in Wistrand 1992.

16. Juvenal, *Satires* 10, 78–81.

17. Fronto, *Letter to His Friends* 2, 3.

18. Suetonius, *Lives of the Twelve Caesars: Augustus*, 70.

19. Seneca, *Dialogues* 11, 17.4.

20. Suetonius, *Lives of the Twelve Caesars: Claudius*, 33.

21. Seneca, *Apocolocyntosis*, 14.

22. See Demandt 1997, 55.

23. I found this text in Wuilleumier 1927, 185–86.

24. I have borrowed this idea from Toner 1995, 92–94. His further calculations are highly speculative.

25. Pliny, *The Natural History* 10, 34.71; I found this reference in Weeber 1994, 54.

26. Cameron 1976. Only minor details of the picture he paints have come in for criticism.

27. Juvenal, *Satires* 11, 199–201: "otherwise you'd see such gloomy faces, such sheer astonishment as greeted the Cannae disaster after our Consuls had bitten the dust."

28. Tertullian, *De spectaculis* 16.

29. Dio Chrysostom, *Discourses* 32, 77.

30. Ibid. 32, 74

31. Suetonius, *Lives of the Twelve Caesars: Augustus*, 45.

32. Suetonius, *Lives of the Twelve Caesars: Caligula*, 55; Cassius Dio, *Roman History* 59, 14.7.

33. Scriptores Historiae Augustae, *Verus*, 4; 6; 10.

34. Suetonius, *Lives of the Twelve Caesars: Nero*, 22.1.

35. Tacitus, *The Annals* 14, 14.2.

36. Suetonius, *Lives of the Twelve Caesars: Nero*, 24.1.

37. Cassius Dio, *Roman History* 73, 17.

38. Ibid. 74, 4.

39. Ibid. 80, 14

40. Scriptores Historiae Augustae, *Heliogabalus*, 23.1; 28.

41. Suetonius, *Lives of the Twelve Caesars: Vitellius*, 4; 7; 14.

42. Cassius Dio, *Roman History* 77, 10; Herodian, *Roman History* 4, 7.2; 4, 11.9; 4, 12.6

43. Marcus Aurelius, *Meditations* 1, 5.

Chapter 8: Changes around the Racetrack

1. Humphrey 1986, 538–39.

2. Ammianus Marcellinus, *Roman History* 28, 4.

3. Ibid. 28, 4.29–31.

4. Ibid. 15, 7.2.

5. Ibid. 26, 3.3.

6. Ibid. 28, 1.27 and 29, 3.5.

7. Amphilochus of Iconium, *Seleucus*, 158–65, 179; I found this text in Dickie 2003, 294.

8. Ammianus Marcellinus, *Roman History* 28, 4.33.

9. *Corpus Inscriptionum Latinarum* 6, 10060.

10. Whitby 1999, 236–39.

11. Liebeschuetz 2001, 211.

12. Monophysitism was the teaching that in the person of the incarnated Christ only divine and therefore no human nature had been present.

13. Procopius, *Secret History*, 7.8–25.

Chapter 9: The Heroes of the Hippodrome

1. Most of the known facts about Porphyrius can be found in the impressive *Porphyrius the Charioteer* by Alan Cameron, published in 1973. With the patience of a monk and with great attention to detail he analyzed the epigrams about the life of Porphyrius and put the texts into the correct order. In the main I have based my reconstruction of the life of Porphyrius and his fellow charioteers on the conclusions drawn by Cameron.

2. John Malalas, *Chronicle*, 395–96; see Cameron 1973, 150.

3. *Anthologia Palatina* 16, 344.

4. *Corpus Inscriptionum Latinarum* 6, 10050.

5. Ibid. 6, 10048.

6. *Anthologia Palatina* 16, 338.

7. *Anthologia Palatina* 16, 354. Nemesis was originally the personification of the task of all the gods to maintain the balance between the world order and the overconfidence of human beings. In late antiquity Nemesis became the goddess of fate, worshiped by soldiers, gladiators, and charioteers.

8. Ibid. 15, 47.

9. Ibid. 16, 350.

10. Ibid. 16, 358.

11. I base this on Cameron 1973, 178–79, who also cites examples of modern jockeys who continued to achieve stunning victories in their late fifties. For a counterargument, see Horsmann 1998, 296.

12. See www.horseracing.about.com/cs/trainersjockeys/a/aa043003c.htm.

13. *Anthologia Palatina* 16, 358.

Chapter 10: The Disappearance of Chariot Racing

1. *Codex Theodosianus*, 15.5.3.

2. Cassiodorus, *Variae epistulae* 3, 51.

3. Procopius, *Gothic War* 3, 37.

Chapter 11: Ben-Hur

1. Solomon 2001, 202.

2. Wallace has the race take place in Antioch.

3. Humphrey 1986, 83.

4. Junkelmann in Köhne, Ewigleben, and Jackson 2000, 90–91.

actionarius	imperial superintendent of the racing stables in Constantinople
agitator	fully trained charioteer
auriga	charioteer
biga	two-horse chariot
carceres	starting stalls
conditor	member of staff of a faction, confidant to the charioteers
Consualia	ancient equestrian festival for the god Consus
decemiuga	ten-horse chariot
diversium	single combat between champions in a two-part race
dominus factionis	head of a racing stable
erupit et vicit	the winner held second place for a long time before passing the leader just before the finishing line
euripus	double dividing wall down the center of the arena with a pool of water in the middle
factio	racing stable; supporters' group attached to a racing stable
factio albata	the Whites
factio aurata	the Golds
factio prasina	the Greens
factio purpurea	the Purples
factio russata	the Reds
factio veneta	the Blues
factionarius	leader of a racing stable from the third century onward
familia quadrigaria	association of *quadriga* drivers
funalis	trace horse

hippagogus	ship specially furnished for the transportation of horses
hortator	member of staff of a faction who passed on orders from the stable to the horses on the racetrack
introiuga	yoke horse
iugalis	yoke horse
kathisma	emperor's loge in the Hippodrome at Constantinople
Ludus	festival with one or more days reserved for chariot racing
mappa	white starting flag
meta	turning point
milliarius	"thousander," a charioteer with more than a thousand victories to his name
morator	stable lad who made the horses comfortable and flung open the doors to the starting stalls
octoiuga	eight-horse chariot
occupavit et vicit	the winner was in the lead from start to finish
pedibus ad quadrigam	race in which the drivers had to sprint for several laps after crossing the finishing line
pompa circensis	opening ceremony
praemia maiora	first prizes
praemissus	charioteer who was sent ahead as a pacesetter and later fell back
pulvinar	emperor's loge in the Circus Maximus
quadriga	four-horse chariot
seiuga	six-horse chariot
sellarius	stable lad
sparsor	member of staff of a faction who sprinkled the horses and drivers with water
spina	dividing wall down the center of the arena
successit et vicit	the winner emerged from the back of the pack
triga	three-horse chariot

SELECTED BIBLIOGRAPHY

This list includes only those books and articles that I consulted regularly in the preparation of this volume. Publications on smaller, more specific issues have been included only if I made extensive use of them.

Aldrete, G. S. *Gestures and Acclamations in Ancient Rome*. Baltimore 1999.

Audollent, A. *Defixionum tabellae*. Paris 1904.

Auguet, R. *Cruelty and Civilization: The Roman Games*. London 1972 (English translation of *Cruauté et civilisation: Les jeux romains*, Paris 1970).

Balsdon, J. P. V. D. *Life and Leisure in Ancient Rome*. London 1969.

Beacham, R. C. *Spectacle Entertainments of Early Imperial Rome*. New Haven 1999.

Bernstein, F. *Ludi Publici: Untersuchungen zur Entstehung und Entwicklung der öffentlichen Spiele im republikanischen Rom*. Stuttgart 1998.

Bury, J. B. *History of the Later Roman Empire from the Death of Theodosius I to the Death of Justinian*. New York 1958.

Cameron, A. *Bread and Circuses: The Roman Emperor and His People*. Oxford 1974.

———. *Circus Factions: Blues and Greens in Rome and Byzantium*. Oxford 1976.

———. *Porphyrius the Charioteer*. Oxford 1973.

Carcopino, J. *Het dagelijks leven in het oude Rome*. Utrecht 1987 (Dutch translation of *La vie quotidienne à Rome à l'apogée de l'Empire*, Paris 1939).

Crouwel, J. H. *Chariots and Other Means of Land Transport in Bronze Age Greece*. Amsterdam 1981.

———. *Chariots and Other Wheeled Vehicles in Iron Age Greece*. Amsterdam 1992.

Crowther, N. B. "Sports Violence in the Roman and Byzantine Empires: A Modern Legacy." *International Journal of Sports* 13 (1996): 445–58.

Demandt, A. *Das Privatleben der römischen Kaiser.* Munich 1997.

Dickie, M. W. *Magic and Magicians in the Greco-Roman World.* London 2003.

Duncan-Jones, R. *The Economy of the Roman Empire: Quantitative Studies.* Cambridge 1982.

Friendländer, L. *Darstellungen aus der Sittengeschichte Roms in der Zeit von August bis zum Ausgang der Antonine.* Vol. 2. Leipzig 1921.

———. *Sittengeschichte Roms.* Cologne 1957.

Gager, J. G. *Curse Tablets and Binding Spells from the Ancient World.* Oxford 1992.

Greatrex, G. "The Nika Riot: A Reappraisal." *Journal of Hellenic Studies* 117 (1997): 60–86.

Harris, H. A. *Sport in Greece and Rome.* Ithaca, NY 1972.

Heucke, C. *Circus und Hippodrom als politischer Raum.* Hildesheim 1994.

Heuts, L. F. "Het Romeinse wagenrennen: Een onderzoek naar de professionele wagenmenner." Ph.D. diss., University of Amsterdam, 2001.

Hönle, A., and A. Henze. *Römische Amphitheater und Stadien.* Zürich 1981.

Horsmann, G. *Die Wagenlenker der römischen Kaiserzeit.* Stuttgart 1998.

Humphrey, J. H. *Roman Circuses: Arenas for Chariot Racing.* Berkeley 1986.

Hyland, A. *Equus: The Horse in the Roman World.* London 1990.

———. *The Horse in the Ancient World.* Gloucestershire 2003.

Junkelmann, M. *Die Reiter Roms.* Pt. 1, *Reise, Jagd, Triumph und Circusrennen.* Mainz am Rhein 1990.

Köhne, E., C. Ewigleben, and R. Jackson, eds. *Gladiators and Caesars: The Power of Spectacle in Ancient Rome.* London 2000.

Liebeschuetz, J. H. W. G. *The Decline and Fall of the Roman City.* Oxford 2001.

Mancioli, D. *Vita e costumi dei Romani antichi.* Pt. 4, *Giochi e spettacoli.* Rome 1987.

Nippel, W. *Public Order in Ancient Rome.* Cambridge 1995.

Potter, D. S., and D. J. Mattingly, eds. *Life, Death and Entertainment in the Roman Empire.* Ann Arbor, MI 1999.

Rawson, E. "Chariot-Racing in the Roman Republic." In *Roman Culture and Society: Collected Papers,* 389–407. Oxford 1991.

Roueché, C. *Performers and Partisans at Aphrodisias.* London 1993.

Solomon, J. *The Ancient World in the Cinema.* New Haven 2001.

Thuillier, J.-P. *Sport im antiken Rom.* Darmstadt 1999.

Toner, J. P. *Leisure and Ancient Rome.* Cambridge 1995.

Vanoyeke, V. *La naissance des Jeux Olympiques et le sport dans l'antiquité.* Paris 1992.

Weeber, K.-W. *Panem et circenses: Massenunterhaltung als Politik im antiken Rom.* Mainz am Rhein 1994.

Wegener Sleeswyk, A. *Wielen, wagens, koetsen.* Leeuwarden 1992.

Whitby, M. "The Violence of the Circus Factions." In *Organised Crime in Antiquity,* edited by K. Hopwood, 229–53. London 1999.

Wistrand, M. *Entertainment and Violence in Ancient Rome: The Attitudes of Roman Writers in the First Century A.D.* Göteborg 1992.

Wuilleumier, P. "Cirque et astrologie." *Mélanges d'archéologie et d'histoire* 44 (1927): 184–209.

INDEX

Page numbers in bold indicate illustrations

acrobats, 29, 74
actors, 83, 114–15, 116, 117, 133, 134
Aeserninus, 74
Africa Proconsularis, 49
Alcibiades, 21
Alcmene, 19
Alexander the Great, 129
Alexandria, 130
Alpheus River, 19
Ammianus Marcellinus, 131–33
Amphilochus of Iconium, 133
Anastasius, 9, 11, 138–39, 140, 142, 144, 146–47
Anthologia Palatina, 149
Antinoopolis, 50, 130
Antioch, 50, 51, 130, 138, 139
Antiquities of the Jews (Flavius Josephus), 98
Antoninus Pius, 36, 50, 127
Apollo, 30
Apronianus, 132
Arch of Titus, 35
Ares, 19
aristocracy/elite: betting by, 109; charioteers from, 52; and Circus Maximus, 31; and common people, 2; and gambling, 111; and horses, 53; income of, 93; and Justinian, 5; at Olympia, 26; and Olympics, 21; and popular theater, 115; as spectators, 1, 2, 3; and support for stables, 55. *See also* knights; senators
Arles, 50
Asinius Pollio, 74

astrology/zodiac, 44, 110–11
Athanasius, 132–33
Auchenius, 132–33
Augustine of Hippo, 106
Augustus, 32, 34, 41, 44, 46, 74, 109, 120
Aulus Fabricius, 55
Aurelian, 47
Aventine Hill, 28, 29, 31

Basilica di Santa Croce in Gerusalemme, 47
Basilica of St. John Lateran, 44, 45
Belisarius, 12
Ben-Hur (film): 1907, 155; 1925, 155–56; 1959, 42, 154, 155, 156–60
Ben-Hur (stage play), 155
Ben-Hur: A Tale of the Christ (Wallace), 154–55, 159
Bernini, Gian Lorenzo, Fountain of the Four Rivers, 48
Blues (stable), 79, 88, 89, 90, **100**; and astrology, 110; betting on, 111, 112; in Constantinople, 135; and decline of Rome, 152; and emperor, 120; financing of, 152; merger with Reds, 111–12; and Nero, 55; and Porphyrius, 144, 145, 146; and seasons and elements, 54
Blues (supporters): and Caligula, 99; and Caracalla, 125, 126; and ceremony at Hippodrome, 153; in Constantinople, 136; and Lucius Verus, 121; and Marcian, 137; and Nika

Blues (supporters) (*cont.*)
  riot, 6–10, 12; and stables, 99; and
    Theodosius II, 136; violence by, 116,
    138, 139–40; and Vitellius, 125. *See
    also* supporters
Bostra, 50, 130
boxers/boxing, 26, 30
Boyd, Stephen, 156
Britannia, 50
Byzantine Empire, 5, 113
Byzantium, 51

Caecina, 112
Caesarea, 32, 50, 130
Calahorra, 50
Calendar of Philocalus, 52, 72
Caligula: and Circus of Gaius (Caligula)
    and Nero, 46–47; confrontations
    with supporters, 66, 98–99; devotion
    of, 120–21; gambling by, 109; and
    Nero, 122; and number of races per
    day, 72; and Vitellius, 125, 126
Callias, 21
Callidromus (horse), 58
Calliopas. *See* Porphyrius
Calpurnianus, 92, 93
Campus Martius, 54, 67
Canaanites, 15
Cappadocia, 57
Caracalla, 36, 47, 125, 126–27
Carthage, 49
Cassiodorus, 72, 75–76, 151
Cassius Chaerea, 98, 166n4
Cassius Dio, 97, 121
Castel Sant' Angelo, 58
Castor and Pollux, 44
Ceres, 30
Charioteer of Delphi, The, 63, 64
charioteer(s), 59, 62–64, 80, 87, 100,
    104; age of, 84, 145, 147–48; as
    agitator, 62; appearance of, 62, 64;
    aristocratic, 52; as *auriga*, 62; in
    Ben-Hur, 159–60; Caracalla as, 126;
    career of, 84–91; and chariot design,
    62; and citizenship, 89; class of, 31,
    53, 82–84; Commodus as, 122–23;
    in Constantinople, 143; criticism of,
    117; dangers to, 64; decline in Rome,
    150; devotion to, 3, 117; driving

techniques of, 64; epitaph for, 84–85;
    equipment/dress of, 64, 77; in Etru-
    ria, 27, 64; and *familia quadrigaria*,
    85; freedmen as, 3; and gladiators,
    94–95; Greek, 17, 18, 62, 64, 130;
    Heliogabalus as, 125; in Homer, 17–
    18; and honor and rewards, 104; and
    horses, 61; illness of, 88; injury of,
    26, 43, 77–78, 88, 95; as leadership
    of stables, 95; less talented, 85; and
    magic and sorcery, 132–33; as *mil-
    liarius*, 89; names for, 62; Nero as,
    122; and Olympics, 21–22; in open-
    ing ceremony, 67; popularity of, 61,
    94–95; as practitioners of *ars ludicra*,
    83; prestige of, 82; quality of, 54;
    recruitment of, 52–53; reputation of,
    110; Roman, 62, 64; salary for, 151;
    senators as, 84; skill of, 3; slaves as,
    3, 86; souvenirs of, 66; Spanish, 50;
    and stables, 53, 54, 103–5; statues
    of, 44, 46, 63, 64, 88, 141, 142, 143,
    145, 147; status of, 26, 83–84, 141;
    strategy of, 68, 76–77, 79–80, 160;
    supporters of, 81, 94–95, 103–5;
    Tacitus on, 107; training of, 53; as
    unruly, 132; and war chariots, 15,
    16; winners and losers, 80–81. *See
    also* race(s), chariot
chariot(s), 15, 16, 61–62; in *Ben-Hur*,
    158; in burial chamber frescoes,
    26–27; crew of, 15; design of, 15, 16,
    20, 62; Egyptian, 15; high-quality,
    53; in Homer, 17–18; inspection of,
    65; models of, 62; and Olympics, 20;
    racing vs. triumphal, 62, 158; six-
    to ten-horse, 60, 73; in Sophocles,
    23–25; for transportation, 16; war,
    15–16, 20
—, four-horse (*quadrigae*), 21, 53,
    73, 75, 104; charioteer of, 62; and
    Circus Maximus, 43; in Etruria, 27;
    horses required for, 60; and Oenom-
    aus, 19; and Olympics, 20, 22; of
    triumphator, 67
—, three-horse (*trigae*): in Etruria,
    27; in racing program, 73; use of, 60
—, two-horse (*bigae*), 27; charioteer
    of, 62; in Etruria, 27; and Olympics,

20; in racing program, 73; use of, 60

Chiusi, relief from, 27

Christians/Christianity, 37, 66, 102–3, 106, 118–19, 131, 133, 137

Chrysaphius, 137

Church of St. Lawrence, 8

Circus Flaminius, 46, 67

Circus Maxentius, 37, 47–48

Circus Maximus, 3, 32–46, 50, 125, 133; Ammianus Marcellinus on, 132; ceremony at, 80; and Circus Maxentius, 48; and Circus of Gaius (Caligula) and Nero, 46, 47; and decline of Rome, 150; design of, 32, 33–37; expansion of, 53; features of, 37–46; fire at, 34, 35; *metae* (turning points) at, 34, 43, 44, 76, 78, 79; as model, 49, 51, 130; model of, 39; popular opinion at, 1–2, 97–99, 131; records maintained at, 84; seating in, 31, 33, 34–35, 36, 37, 38–40, 41, 66–67, 96; size of, 37–38; and stables, 54, 65; starting gates at, 33, 34, 35, 36, 41, 42, 43, 44; statuary of, 34, 44, 46; symbols indicating laps at, 34, 44; and Tarquinius Priscus, 29; vendors at, 66; and zodiac, 44

Circus of Gaius (Caligula) and Nero (Circus Vaticanus), 46

Circus Varianus, 47, 125

Circus Vaticanus, 46, 122

city cohorts, 81, 101, 115. *See also* police

Cladeus River, 19

class, 96; and betting, 109; of charioteers, 31, 53, 82–84; and Circus Maximus, 35, 39, 41–42; and income, 92–93; of organizers, 53; and Roman population, 30; and stables, 54–55; of supporters, 1–4, 55

Claudius, 35, 47, 72, 76, 109

Claudius Olympus, 148

Cleander, 97

Cleisthenes of Sicyon, 21

Codex Theodosianus, 150

Cologne, 50

Colosseum, 2, 34, 37, 38, 97, 131

Columella, 57

Commodus, 97, 109, 122–23, **124**, 125

common people, 96; Ammianus Marcellinus on, 131; betting by, 109; and Circus Maximus, 31, 35, 39; elite disapproval of, 2, 3, 107, 108; in Homer, 17; imperial control of, 131; Juvenal on, 108; at Olympia, 26; as organizers, 53; political influence of, 1–2, 97–99; rioting by, 97; and support for stables, 55; violence by, 114, 115

Consentius, 69

Constantine, 5, 9, 37, 50, 51

Constantinople, 4; building of Hippodrome at, 51, 135; city militia of, 6; and decline of Rome, 150, 151; riots in, 5, 137, 138, 139; stables in, 54, 130. *See also* Hippodrome

Constantinus, 140, 143, 148, 149

Constantius II, 37, 44, 45

Consualia, 29

Consus, 29

Corax, 76

Corinth, 18

cosmos, 44, 46

Crescens, 85, 145

Cronus, 19

Crusaders, 142, 153

curse tablets, 101–3, 111, 114

Cybele, 30, 44

Cyprian, 66

Cyrnus, 79

Delphi, 18, 22, 23, 26, 51

Didius Julianus, 109

Dio Chrysostom, 119

Diocletian, 36, 51, 129

Dionysius of Halicarnassus, 33, 34, 38

Domitian, 32, 72, 86, 96, 99; and Circus Maxentius, 48; and Circus Maximus, 35; gambling by, 109; presence at races, 42

Egypt/Egyptians, 15, 16, 20, 44, 49, 50

Electra (Sophocles), 23–25

Elis, 19

Empedocles of Acragas, 21

emperor(s), 3, 84, 96; as arbiter between organizers and stables, 55; and ceremony at Hippodrome, 137, emperors (*cont.*)

152, 153; Christian, 37, 131; and circuses outside Italy, 49, 50; and Circus Maximus, 36, 41–42; control of common people by, 131; and control of spectator violence, 116; and decline of Rome, 152; financing of races by, 152; gambling by, 109–10; good vs. bad, 120, 127, 128; loge of, 6, 8, 12, 36, 41; and popular opinion, 1, 5–6, 97–99; and provision of horses, 73; and public in Constantinople, 135–40; at races, 41–42, 96–97; and riots, 117–18; and stables, 135; and supporters, 100–101, 117, 120–27, 134, 136–37; and violence among spectators, 117–18; and winning charioteer, 81

Epaphroditus, 86

Equirria, 29

Etruria/Etruscans, 26–28, 52, 64

Eutyches of Tarraco, 88–89

Eutychus, 121

Faustinus, 140, 143, 148

Felix, 103

festivals, 1, 18, 31, 52, 66; centenary, 72; early Roman, 29–30; in eastern Roman Empire, 129; financing of, 130; and Roman Empire, 32

Flavius Josephus, 98

Flavius Scorpus, 77–78, 89, 91, 93–94

Flora, 30

Florus, 78

Forum Boarium, 34, 67

Forum Romanum, 32, 35, 47, 67

François vase, 17

Fulvius Nobilior, 34

Gaius Appuleius Diocles, 50, 58, 89, 90–92, 93, 111, 145, 148

Gaius Flaminius, 46

Gaius Stertinus, 34

Garfield, James, 155

gates/starting gates, 22, 46, 49, 56; at Circus Maximus, 33, 34, 35, 36, 41, 42, 43, 44

Gaul, 49, 50, 58

Gerasa, 50, 51, 130

Germania, 50

Geta, 126–27

gladiators/gladiator shows: appeal of, 30; days for, 52; decline of, 37, 130–31; as disreputable, 83; and gambling, 110; organization of, 32, 49; popularity of, 94–95; and prestige of empire, 129

gods, 18, 67. *See also* mythology; religion

Golds (stable), 99

Gortyn, 50

Greece, 14, 51, 58, 159; war chariots in, 15–16

Greeks, 17–18, 52; charioteers of, 62, 64; and eastern Roman Empire, 129–30. *See also* Olympic Games

Greens (stable), 79, 88, 89, 90, 110, 111, 112; and Caligula, 120; in Constantinople, 135; and emperor, 120; financing of, 152; and Nero, 55; and Porphyrius, 144, 145, 146; and seasons and elements, 54

Greens (supporters), 99, 114, 116; in Constantinople, 135, 137, 138, 139–40; and emperors, 46, 99, 121, 122–23, 125–26, 136, 137; and Hippodrome ceremony, 153; and Nika riot, 6–10, 12; rioting by, 136, 137, 138, 139–40

Hadrian, 89, 127, 130

Hadrumetum, 49

Hagia Sophia, 9, 13

Heliogabalus, 47, 66, 125

Heliopolis, 44

Herakles, 19

Heston, Charlton, 156

Hiero of Syracuse, 21

Hilarinus, 132

Hilarus (horse), 58

Hippodamia, 19

Hippodrome, 74, 135, 136; appearance of, 141–42; and Constantine, 51; dimensions of, 5, 6; fire at, 9, 138, 142; imperial ceremony at, 137, 152, 153; and Nika riot, 12, 152; as political barometer, 5–6; *spina* at, 141, 142, 143; violence in, 5, 6, 8, 12, 13, 139

History of Rome (Livy), 28, 29, 33
Hittites, 15, 16
Homer, 17–18, 26, 43
honor, 52, 53, 83
Honorius, 102
horseracing, 26, 28, 29, 33, 67, 74
horse(s), **16**, 44, 56–61, **59**; and aristocracy, 53; availability of, 52, 53, 56; in *Ben-Hur,* 159; breeding and training of, 53, 56, 57, 58–59, 65; of Calpurnianus, 90; care of, 56, 57; and chariot design, 62; dealers in, 57; and Diocles, 91; and Greek chariot design, 20; and Greeks, 16; injuries to, 58–59, 60, 77, 78; for military use vs. racing, 73; names of, 61; of Oenomaus, 19; racing position of, 58, 62; reputation of, 60–61; size of, 57; sources of, 57; speed of, 57; and stables, 53, 54; as status symbols, 14–15; for war chariots, 15
hunting shows, 30, 34, 37, 49
Hypatius, 11, 12

Iliad (Homer), 17–18, 26, 43
Incitatus (horse), 121
Innocent X, 48
Isidore of Seville, 54
Italica, 50
Italy, 26

Jews, 7, 35, 163n2
John Chrysostom, 61
Julianus, 140, 143, 148
Julius Caesar, 31, 34
Junkelmann, Marcus, 158
Juno, 29
Jupiter, 29, 30
Jupiter Capitolinus, 67
Justin I, 142
Justinian, 7, 142, 152; and Nika riot, 5, 6–7, 8, 9, 10–11, 13
Juvenal, 1, 65–66, 93, 107–8, 114, 163n1

knights, 29, 53, 93, 100; and Circus Maximus, 31, 35, 39; and stable organization, 55, 95, 134. *See also* aristocracy/elite
Knossos, 15

Lacerta, 93
Laodicea, 51, 130
Leontius, 132
Leptis Magna (Libya), arena at, 42, 49
Libya, 49, 57
Livy, 28, 29, 33
Longden, Johnny, 148
Lucius Verus, 108, 109, 121
ludi, 29–30, 31
ludi saeculares, 72, 73, 74, 76
Lyon, circus at, 50

Macrinus, 128
magic/sorcery, 101, 132–33
magistrates, 9, 29, 49, 50, 52, 53, 75
Mainz, 50
Malalas, John, 144
Manichaeans, 7, 163n2
Marcian, 137
Marcus Aurelius, 108, 121, 122, 127
Marcus Aurelius Mollicius Tatianus, 88
Marcus Aurelius Polyneices, 88
Marcus Cornelius Fronto, 108–9
Marcus Valerius Maximus, 33
Mars, 29
Martial, 60–61, 77–78, 93–94, 96, 107–8
Maxentius, 37, 47
Maximinus, 132–33
Maximinus the Thracian, 128
Mérida, 50
Messia, 44
Middle East, 14, 15
Milan, 51, 129
Miltiades, 21
Minerva, 29
Monophysitism, 138, 168n12
Monte Pincio Park, 47
Mundus, 12
Murcia River valley, 28, 29
Mussolini, Benito, 156
Mycenaeans, 15, 16
Myron of Sicyon, 21
mythology, 44, 61. *See also* gods; religion

Narses, 12
Near East, 15
Nemea, 18, 51
Nemesis, 145, 169n7

Neptune, 29, 44
Nero, 47, **123**, 148; and actors, 115; as arbiter between organizers and stables, 55; as charioteer, 106–7, 122; devotion of, 121–22; gambling by, 109; and number of races per day, 72; and Poppaea Sabina, 122; and rebuilding of Circus Maximus, 35; and starting procedure, 76
Niblo, Fred, 155
Nicomedia, 51, 129
Nika riot, 5–13, 14, 137, 148, 152
Nonius Asprenas, 74
North Africa, 49, 57, 58, 101–2, 144

obelisks, 37, 44, 45, 46–47, 48, 142
Oenomaus of Pisa, 19
Olcott, Sidney, 155
Olympia, 18, 19, 20–23, 51, 122, 159
Olympic Games, 18–26, 122, 159. See also Greeks
Orestes, 23
On Horsemanship (Xenophon), 56–57
organizers: competition among, 54; and financing of races, 52, 53; in opening ceremony, 67; and payment to stable directors, 55; and prizes, 81, 94; of provincial circuses, 85; and stables, 134, 135
Ovid, 40–41, 68–69, 76, 99

Palatine Hill, 28, 29, 31, 32
Palazzo Barberini, 47
Palazzo della Cancelleria, 54
Palestine, 49, 50
Panvinio, Onofrio, 142
Papirius Dionysius, 97
Pausanias, 19–20, 22
Pelagonius, 57, 77
Peloponnesos peninsula, 19
Pelops, 19
Pertinax (consul), 123, 125
Pertinax (horse), 123, 125
Philoromus, 132
Phocas, 153
Phrygia, 30
Piazza del Popolo, 44, 47
Piazza di Porta Capena, 32
Piazza Farnese, 54

Piazza Navona, 38, 48
Pincay, Laffit, Jr., 148
Pliny the Elder, 39, 57, 76, 78, 112
Pliny the Younger, 3, 35–36, 105–6, 107, 108
police, 8, 9, 115, 137, 138. See also city cohorts; Praetorian Guard
Polyneices, 88
Polyphemus, 135
Pompeius, 11
Pompeius Musclosus, 89, 91, 148
Poppaea Sabina, 122
Porphyrius, 140, 142–49
Porta Libitinaria, 43
Porta Triumphalis, 67
Portugal, 50
Praetorian Guard, 81, 97, 101, 107, 115. See also city cohorts; police
prizes/prize money, 60, 104; amounts of, 85, 91–95; and class of charioteers, 85–86; and decline of Rome, 150; division of, 86–87; in Homer, 17–18; and honor, 83; for horse vs. chariot races, 74; Martial on, 108; and Panhellenic festivals, 18; and professional spectacles, 53; reception of, 81
Probus, 9
Procopius, 11, 12, 139–40
procurators, 93
prostitution, 66
Publius Aelius Calpurnianus Gutta, 89–90
Punic War, Second, 30
Purples (stable), 99
Pylos, 15–16
Pythian Games, 22, 23

race(s), chariot, **113**; accounts of, 68–72; betting on, 109–12; ceremonial procession for, 67; course of, 77; diversium, 74, 149; entertainments between, 73–74; false starts in, 76; finish of, 79–80; hazards of, 77–78, 80; intervals between, 81; kinds of, 73, 74–75; laps of, 23, 34, 44; length of, 67–68; and mappa (white flag), 75–76; number in day's program, 60, 72–73, 152; number of days held, 96; pedibus ad quadrigam, 74–75; as professionally produced spectacles, 53; and sabotage and threats, 75; social disorder after, 81; speeds in, 68; and starting procedure at Circus Maximus, 33, 42–43, 56, 75–76; and starting procedure at Olympia, 22–23, 42; and starting procedure in Homer, 17, 18; time of, 68; winners and losers of, 80–81. See also charioteer(s); horseracing

race track(s), 49; in Ben-Hur, 158; of Circus Maximus, 33, 42; early Roman, 28–29; in Etruria, 27; in Homer, 17, 18; length of Hippodrome, 5; length of various, 161; list of, 161; at Olympia, 20–21, 22–23, 26; preparation of, 81

Ramses II, 44

Ratumenna of Veii, 27–28

Re (Egyptian sun god), 44

Reds (stable), 79, 88, 89, 90, 91, 103; and Anastasius, 140; and astrology, 110; betting on, 111, 112; in Constantinople, 135–36, 140; and emperor, 120; merger with Blues, 111–12; and Nero, 55; and seasons and elements, 54

Reds (supporters), 99

religion, 29, 31. See also gods; mythology

Robert of Clari, 142

Rome: conquests by, 53; decline of, 128–29, 131, 150–51; decline of racing in, 150; early growth in population of, 30; early racing in, 28–31; financial resources of, 152; racing in imperial, 32; social hierarchy of, 1–4

Roman History (Ammianus Marcellinus), 131–33

Romulus, 28, 29, 33

Sabines, Rape of, 28

sacrifice, 67

Saguntum, 50

Saintes, circus at, 50

Samaritans, 7, 163n2

Santiago do Cacém, 32, 50

San Vitale, Church of (Ravenna), 7

satyrs, 67

Scipio Africanus, 79

Scirtus, 88

seasons, 44, 54

seating: in Ben-Hur, 158; capacity of, 38–39; and circus at Antioch, 51; and Circus Maxentius, 48; at Circus Maximus, 31, 33, 34–35, 36, 37, 38–40, 41, 66–67, 96; and class, 31, 35, 39; collapse of, 36; in Colosseum, 40; and Constantine, 37; and hunting shows, 34; at Leptis Magna, 49; and Olympia Hippodrome, 20; and Tarquinius Priscus, 29. See also spectators

Seia, 44

senators: Ammianus Marcellinus on, 131; as charioteers, 84; at Circus Maximus, 31, 35, 39; and emperors, 128; and Hippodrome, 6; horses of, 53; income of, 93; leisure time of, 2; as supporters, 100–101, 109; and Tarquinius Priscus, 29. See also aristocracy/elite

Seneca, 3, 93, 107, 109

Septimius Severus, 5, 73, 74

Sessorium, 47

Sicily, 57

Sidonius Apollinaris, 69–72

sileni, 67

Silius Italicus, 79

Sirmium, 51, 129

Sixtus V, 44

slaves, 82, 83, 86, 96, 150–51

Sophocles, 23–25

Spain, 49, 50, 57, 58

spectators, 94; and Antioch circus, 51; and Circus Maxentius, 48; and Circus Maximus, 31, 32, 33, 37, 38–39; class of, 1, 31, 39, 41; and Colosseum, 38; commotion of, 65–66; emotions of, 3, 118–19; and emperor, 41–42, 96–97; in Etruria, 27; and finish of race, 81; and Hippodrome, 6; in Homer, 17; at Olympia, 20, 26; perspective of, 79; political voice of, 34, 97–98; and Tarquinius Priscus, 29; Tertullian on, 118–19; view of, 36; violence by, 81. See also seating; supporters *spina:* in *Ben-Hur,* 158; at Circus Maxentius, 48; at Circus Maximus, 37, 39, 41, 43, 44, 45, 46, 76; at Circus of Gaius (Caligula) and Nero, 47; at Circus Varianus, 47; at Hippodrome, 141, 142, 143; at Leptis Magna, 49; and race, 77; and race strategy, 68

stable(s): *actionarius* (financial administrator) of, 135; and *Ben-Hur,* 159; betting on, 111–12; change in function of, 134–35; charioteers' relationship to, 103–5; colors of, 54; competition among, 54; *conditores* of, 56; in Constantinople, 135–36; *dominus factionis* of, 55, 134, 135; in eastern Roman Empire, 130; and emperors, 135, 137; financing by, 130; *hortatores* of, 56, 79, 149; *moratores* of, 56, 75, 76; organization of, 55; and organizers, 134, 135; origin of, 53; and prize money, 86–88; professional employees of, 55–56; public support for, 54–55; reputation of, 54; responsibility in late antiquity, 135; *sellarii* of, 56; souvenirs of, 66; *sparsores* of, 56; strategy involving drivers for, 85; supporters' relationship to, 99–105; *tentores* of, 56

Stadium of Domitian, 37–38
St. Mark's Basilica, Venice, 142
St. Peter's Basilica, Rome, 46
St. Peter's Square, Rome, 46, 47
Subrius Flavus, 107
Suetonius, 66, 74, 120, 125
Sulla, 31
Sultanahmet Square, 141
supporters: Ammianus Marcellinus on, 131–32; Augustine on, 106; charioteers' relationship to, 103–5; class of, 1–4, 55; and decline of Rome, 152; devotion of, 101, 103, 105; and districts or streets, 99; in eastern Roman Empire, 130; and emperors, 100, 134, 136–37; emperors as, 117, 120–27; fanaticism of, 101; and Greek model, 130; and horses, 60–61; and Nika riot, 6–13; numbers of, 1; paid clappers as, 133–34, 136;

Pliny the Younger on, 105–6, 107, 108; rioting by, 101, 112–19, 132, 133, 136, 137–40, 153; and slaves as charioteers, 86; and stables, 99–105; Tacitus on, 106–7; and trade associations, 99–100; violence by, 55, 101, 133–34. *See also* spectators
Syria, 49, 50

Tacitus, 3, 106–7, 122
Tarquinius Priscus, 28–29, 33
Tarquinius Superbus, 27, 29–30, 33
Tarragona, 50
Temple of Jupiter Optimus Maximus, 27, 28, 29–30
Temple of Venus Obsequens, 34
Teres, 58
Tertullian, 54, 118–19, 165n1
Thallus, 93
theater: financial administration of, 135; paid clappers in, 133; popular Roman, 30; in Roman authors, 116, 117; and Roman calendar, 52; and Roman empire, 32; and Roman *ludi,* 30; and violence, 114–15, 118, 138, 139
Theater of Marcellus, 37, 46, 97
Theater of Pompey, 46
Theoderik, 151
Theodora, **10**, 11
Theodosius I, 102, 142, **143**
Theodosius II, 136, 137
Thutmose III, 15, 44
Thysdrus, 49
Tiberius, 120
Tiberius Gracchus, 30
Tiberius II, 152, 153
Titus, 35, 72
Tomba della Olimpiadi, 27
Tomba delle Bighe, 27
Totila, 151
Trajan, 35–36, 37, 42, 43, 127, 130, 148
Trier, 50, 51, 129
Trojan Game, 73–74
Turkey, 15, 57
Tutankhamun, 20
Tyre, 51, 130

umpire(s), 20, 42, 48, 75, 76, 160
Uranius, 143, 148
Utica, 49

Valentinianus, 132
Vatican, 47
Veii, 27–28
Velabrum, 67
Vespasian, 47, 72
veterinarians, 56, 57, 58–59, 65, 77
Via Appia, 37, 47
Via della Conciliazione, 46
Via Flaminia, 89
Via Sacra, 67
Victoria, goddess of victory, 31, 44
Vienne, 50
Vitalianus, 146
Vitellius, 109, 125–26
Volucer (horse), 121

Wallace, Lew, 154–55, 159
war, 15, 16, 52, 53
Whites (stable), 79, 88, 89, 90; and astrology, 110; betting on, 111, 112; in Constantinople, 135, 140; and emperor, 120; merger with Greens, 111–12; and Nero, 55; and seasons and elements, 54
Whites (supporters), 99
women, 22, 27, 40, 66, 95, 166n2
Wyler, William, 156

Xenophon, 56–57

Zeno, 138
Zeus, 19
Zeuxippus, Baths of, 9